Human Development Capability Poverty:

Assessment and its Relationship with Income Poverty

Dr. Rajendra Kumar Jain

M.Com. M.Phil. Ph.D
Lecturer in Economic Administration and
Financial Management
Government College, Nasirabad

Dr. Bharti Jain

M.Sc. Hons. Ph. D
Associate Professor
Department of Foods and Nutrition
Maharshi Dayanand Saraswati University, Ajmer

SCIENTIFIC PUBLISHERS (INDIA)

P.O. BOX 91 JODHPUR

Published by:
Pawan Kumar
Scientific Publishers (India)
5-A, New Pali Road,
P.O. Box 91
Jodhpur - 342 001
E-mail: info@scientificpub.com
www.scientificpub.com

ISBN: 978-81-7233-544-1

Cover design: Tanay Sharma

Lasertype set: Rajesh Ojha
Printed in India

PREFACE AND ACKNOWLEDGMENT

This book presents the current position pertaining to human capability in Tonk district of Rajasthan disaggregated by gender and place of residence. The main objective of the present study is to undertake a situation analysis of the variables of capability poverty. The three variables employed in the study to measure capability poverty cover substantial ground of social sector. The proportion of underweight children indicates the state of health and nutrition for the population as a whole. Access to reproductive health and general services has been provided by the variable of unattended births. Female adult illiteracy has been taken to assess basic educational attainment plus information on gender inequality.

In spite of quite satisfactory progress in gross domestic product and per capita income, India has failed to develop even minimum essential capabilities of its people. The level of human capabilities is less than that of other developing countries with similar per capita income. There are wide female-male and rural-urban disparities for human capability development. Nearly one-third of the population continues to live with meager resources and incomes barely enough to replenish daily individual nutritional requirements. The gains of development are not evenly distributed among various sections of society. More than fifty years after independence, the level of poverty has not declined.

Due to poor human capability, the productivity and competitiveness of Indian economy are significantly low and are likely to perpetuate as nearly 61.5 per cent of the population suffer from capability poverty. These people neither have adequate food, nor access to facilities like education, health care, water, sanitation and shelter.

With adult illiteracy rate of 48 per cent, the country harbours more than 50 per cent of the world's illiterates. The adult literacy rate for male and female (1995) is 65.5 and 37.7 per cent respectively. The mean year of schooling for 25 years and above is as low as 2.4 years, against 12 and 4 years respectively, for developed and developing countries. Forty-five million of the children do not go to primary school. Indeed, there are a large number of children outside school today than there were in 1911. The dropout rate from schools reaches 70 per cent by the time children reach class ten. The numbers of child workers in the age group of 5-14 are estimated to be 11.3 million out of them 5.1 million are female child workers. Despite having the third largest bank of skilled personnel in the world, India faces the prospect of going into the twenty-first century with the deadweight of about 300 million illiterate adults. Also the availability of scientific and technical (SST) manpower-per-thousand people are only 3.5 against 85 and 9 for the developed and developing countries, respectively.

Indicators for health also look bad. The life expectancy is 61 as compared to 67 for developing countries as a whole. The lack of health infrastructure is reflected in our relatively high mortality rates. The infant and under-five mortality rate (1996) are 73 and 111 respectively. About one-third of the infants are low-birth weight and more than half of the children under-age five are underweight. It is highly shocking that about 88 per cent of the pregnant women aged 15-49 suffer from anaemia and two-thirds of the births are unattended by trained health personnel. The maternal mortality rate (per 1,00,000 live births) is 570. The proportion of people without access to safe water (1990-96) is 19 per cent. About 15 per cent of the population (1990-95) does not have access to health services. Almost 71 per cent of the population (1990-96) lives without access to sanitation facilities.

The yields on capital are quite low. The incremental capital-output ratio (ICOR), which has lower values for more efficient economies, is as high as 4 to 6 in India. The quality of personnel, entrepreneurship and management reveals inherent weaknesses of the economy to compete with others.

Nobel laureate Prof. Amartya Sen has said that the basic problem with India is that it has ignored education, health care and other aspects of "social opportunity building."

Rajasthan is one of the least developed states of India in terms of many socio-economic and demographic indicators. Tonk district, the survey area of the project is one of the least developed districts of Rajasthan. The results of the study point to the high prevalence of capability deprivation, particularly in rural areas and call for immediate and special attention of the policy makers.

The book contains invaluable information about indicators of health, education and gender inequality such as underweight children, female adult illiteracy and unattended births. Never before in India has such a study on capability poverty been undertaken. I do hope that it will contribute to the knowledge of researchers and useful to the policy makers.

The study on 'capability poverty' could not have been successfully completed without cooperation and support from innumerable sources at various stages of the project. Although it is not possible to individually acknowledge everyone, several persons and organizations deserve special attention.

Our special thanks are due to the University Grants Commission, Zonal Office, Bhopal for permission and providing the necessary financial assistance to carry out this project.

We are highly thankful to the library staff of Jawahar Lal Nehru University, New Delhi; University of Rajasthan, Jaipur and M.D.S. University, Ajmer for their permission to consult the library. We record our gratitude to the library staff of Govt. College, Ajmer.

Last but not least, the credit goes to the household respondents who spent their time and responded to the rather lengthy questionnaires with tremendous patience.

Though we have put in our sincere efforts with full devotion in completion of this study, yet we beg to be excused for any shortcomings and errors.

Dr. Rajendra Kumar Jain
Dr. Bharti Jain

LIST OF TABLES

LIST OF FIGURES

CONTENTS

Chapter 1

INTRODUCTION

CAPABILITY POVERTY AND HUMAN DEVELOPMENT

India, since 1990 is fleeting through a phase of intense economic, social and political transformations and these changes have important impact on human development parameters such as access to mass education and primary health care. The new economic environment is redefining the role of government and its commitment to social sector development.

1.1 CAPABILITY POVERTY

1.1.1 Human Capability

The real wealth of a nation is its people and they are born with certain potentialities. This simple but powerful truth is too often forgotten in the pursuit of material and financial wealth. The purpose of development is to create an environment in which all people can expand their capabilities and enjoy long, healthy and creative lives. Development must enable all individuals to enlarge their human capabilities to the fullest and to put those capabilities to the best use in all fields-economic, social, cultural and political.

A development approach aims to provide equity in opportunity that however, does not mean the equity in final achievements. Each individual is entitled to a just opportunity to make the best use of his or her potential capabilities. So is each generation. How they actually use these opportunities, and the results they achieve, is a matter of their own choice.

The levels of capabilities that individuals attain depend on many circumstances over which they may not have much control. For example, the food may lead the infants to be underweight that is totally beyond their control. Similarly, if a girl faces discrimination early in life-because she is fed less than her brothers, is sent to school later or not at all or is subjected to physical abuse-the scars (poor development of potential capabilities) she suffers may last all her life and may even be transferred to her offspring. It may happen, in fact rarely that a child who is not sent to school, is not taught any skills or is not given much support still does well due to unusual initiative, ability or luck. But the cards are stacked very firmly against that child.

In India, a vast layer of the populace is plagued by the lack of education, and has little access to health and nutrition. Among the most important reasons for the sluggish progress regarding formation of human capabilities is the low level of spending by both the centre and states on social sectors including health, family welfare and education and lack of political and bureaucratic commitment. India barely spends 5.3 per cent of GDP on essential health and education services, and the expenditure on family welfare is just one per cent of GDP.

Health and knowledge are essential components of human well - being. Improvements in health or education are regarded as valuable in their own right, whether they increase production or not. Human capabilities, such as health or knowledge, are more than means of achieving human well-being. As capabilities are ends in themselves, certain investment for their formation and expansion is always welcome even if conventional economic rates of return turn out to be zero. The object of formation of capabilities is applicable to all members of society including the old, the infirm, the chronically sick and those with disabilities.

The human capabilities that are the focus of human development are broader than productive abilities. Although capabilities do result in increased productivity and income, but these are of value only if they genuinely add to human well-being.

Expansion of capabilities results in peoples' basic empowerment. Capability expansion involves an enlargement of choices and thus an increase in freedom. For example, everyone may be free to read a newspaper, but exercising this freedom depends on literacy. Likewise, everyone may be free to travel around the country, but not if bedridden with illness.

1.1.2 Basic Capabilities

Expansion of capabilities is the main focus of Human development. Different from income, capabilities are ends, and they are reflected not in inputs, but in human outcomes-in the quality of people's lives. Following are considered to be basic human capabilities:

1. Leading a life free of morbidity. Failure reflects in ill health.
2. Being informed and educated. Failure reflects in illiteracy.
3. Being well nourished. Failure reflects in low weight.

Another basic capability, one all too often ignored, is healthy reproduction.

1.1.3 Capability Poverty

Capability poverty is the deprivations reflected in a lack of basic capabilities-when people are unable to reach a certain level of essential human achievement or functioning. Lack of opportunity is largely accountable for the capability poverty. It signifies that society has not provided people with access to the means to develop or maintain essential human capabilities. For example, adequate health services might not be available to ensure that people are protected against avoidable morbidity, or schooling might not be available to ensure literacy and numeracy. Capability poverty tends to be more prevalent in rural areas because of the low coverage of basic education and health services.

It is the responsibility of society, or of government as its representative to remove the barriers to access and to ensure that access is not merely potential or formal. Reckoning that human deprivation occurs in a number of critical dimensions and is not confined to lack of income alone, there was a need for developing a more people centred measure of deprivation. To this direction, the Capability Poverty Measure (CPM) was devised as a multi-dimensional index of poverty focused on capabilities.

1.1.4 What is the Capability Poverty Measure?

The Capability Poverty Measure (CPM) is a multidimensional measure of human deprivation. Intended to complement income measures of poverty, it focuses on human capabilities, as the human development index does. But rather than examining the average state of people's capabilities, it reflects the percentage of people who lack basic, or minimally essential, human capabilities. The CPM, devised by UNDP, is a simple index composed of three indicators that reflect the percentage of the population with capability shortfalls in three basic dimensions of human development. These are:

1. The capability to be well nourished and healthy-represented by the percentage of children under five years of age, who are underweight.

2. The capability for safe and healthy reproduction-proxied by the percentage of births unattended by trained health personnel.
3. The capability to be educated and knowledgeable-represented by percentage of women aged 15 years and above who are illiterate.

Methodologically, the CPM's three variables are given equal weight in the composite index. This assumes that one basic capability is not a substitute for another that is lacking. For such "foundational" capabilities, this is a reasonable assumption, and it implies that policy should not seek to trade one off against another. However, if flexibility in weights is desired, it can be affected by assigning different weights. For each country these measures are added together and divided by three to give a simple arithmetic mean. The lower this mean, the less the capability poverty. Rather than trying to be comprehensive by reflecting deprivation in all human priority areas, the index emphasises critical areas where progress is needed most. The CPM could also incorporate other variables, but for international comparisons, keeping it simple increases its usefulness.

1.1.5 Human Development

Human development (HD) is a broad and comprehensive concept. It is a process of enlarging people's choices. It covers all human choices in all societies at all stages of human development. Though in principle, the choices can be infinite and can change overtime yet at all levels of development, the three minimally essential choices for people are: to lead a long and healthy life; to acquire knowledge and; to have access to the resources needed for a decent standard of living. If these essential choices are not available, many other opportunities remain inaccessible. HD, however, is not confined to these choices only. Additional choices, highly valued by many people, range from political, economic and social freedom to opportunities for being creative and productive and enjoy personal self respect and guaranteed human rights. The concept of HD does not start with any predetermined model. It draws its inspiration from the long term goals of a society. It weaves development around people, not people around development.

Human Development encapsulates those aspects of human life that contribute to better health, education, welfare and happiness. In international flora and world conferences, the concepts and definitions of HD are changing coupled with increasing focus on its monitoring. There is universal agreement on the need to achieve mass education (especially female education), health care, gender equality, equity and empowerment of women.

Human development consists of two sides. One is the formation of human capabilities-such as improved health, knowledge and skills. The other is the use people make of their acquired capabilities for productive purposes, for leisure or for being active in cultural, social and political affairs. If the scales of human development do not finely balance the two sides, much human frustration can result.

The scope of human development broadens the development dialogue from a discussion of mere means (GNP growth) to a discussion of ultimate ends. It includes not only the generation of economic growth but also its distribution. It is as concerned with basic needs as with the entire spectrum of human aspirations. Similarly, it is overwhelmed with the human distress of the north as well as the human deprivation of the south. The real foundation of human development is universalism in acknowledging the life claims of everyone.

1.1.6 Human Development and Human Capabilities

Human development, as a concept, is broad and comprehensive than human capabilities. HD is guided by a simple idea-people always come first. But it does not focus on social issues at the expense of economic issues. It stresses the need to develop human capabilities. But it is equally concerned with how those capabilities are used-by people who can participate freely in social, political and economic decision making and who can work productively and creatively for development. The emphasis that HD places on human capabilities only because these investments in people are vital, but they are only part of the picture. HD is not limited to social sectors only, such as health and education.

1.1.7 The CPM and the HDI

The capability poverty measure (CPM) differs from the human development Index (HDI) in that it focuses on people's lack of capabilities rather than on the average level of capabilities in a country. In addition, the HDI uses income, but the CPM does not. Comparing results of the CPM with those of the HDI would show that some countries have done relatively better in raising average capabilities than in reducing capability poverty-and others have done relatively better in reducing capability poverty than in raising average capabilities.

1.2 TONK DISTRICT- A PROFILE

Tonk, an erstwhile princely state of Rajasthan is located in its north-eastern part between longitudes 75°07′ and 76°19′ and latitudes 25°41′ and 26°34′. It bound in the north by Jaipur district, in the west by Ajmer district and in the east by Sawai Madhopur district. The present set-up of Tonk district has two sub-divisions. Tonk sub-division comprises tehsils of Uniara, Niwai, Deoli and Tonk while Malpura sub-division has Malpura and Todaraisingh tehsils under its jurisdiction.

With the advent of democratic decentralisation in 1959, six Panchayat Samities were formed in the district. They are guided by the Zila Parishad which functions under the Chairmanship of the Zila Pramukh. The ultimate aim of the

Government is to make the Panchayat Samities the main agencies of all the developmental activities at the block level.

1.2.1 Physiography and Climate

The district is flat and has a shape of a kite. Generally, it has an elevation of about 264.32 metres above sea level. The only important river of the district, Banas, divides it into two halves. The soil is somewhat sandy but fertile. Though the depth of water level in general is not much, but in most of the areas after 20 ft., of underground water level bed rock formations are found with the result that sub-soil water for irrigation is limited.

The climate of the district is dry and healthy. From March onwards the temperature tends to rise and is at peak during May and June. Between the middle of November and January the season is cold. Humidity prevails in the atmosphere during the monsoon season that usually starts in the third week of June and lasts upto the middle of September.

1.2.2 Land-Use

The total geographical area of the district is 716,309 hectares. The reporting area for the land utilisation purposes was 718,814 hectares in 1988-89. About 3.49 per cent of the total area of the district is covered under forests. The soil of the district in general is alluvial but the south-eastern part of the district is sandy. The soil varies from sandy loam to loam in Niwai tehsil and parts of Tonk and other tehsils.

1.2.3 Education

An impressive progress has been made in the field of education after independence. There were 141 Primary

Schools in 1951 and by the end of 1988-89, this number has gone upto 709. Among the schools there were 206 Middle Schools, 66 Higher Secondary Schools besides 3 Colleges for general and one for special and professional education. Facilities for college education exist at Tonk, Deoli and Banasthali. The Banasthali Vidyapith is a premier all-India residential institution for girls.

1.2.4 Medical, Public Health and other Facilities

Medical and health facilities have steadily expanded in the district. In 1988-89 there were 7 General Hospitals, 15 Dispensaries, 20 Primary Health Centres, 2 Mother and Child Welfare Centres. Total number of beds available in these institutions are: General 191, Tuberculosis 20, Eye 14, Pediatric 7, Primary Health Centres 180, Maternity 14, Isolation 20 and M.C.W. 7.

There is poor availability of medical and educational facilities in rural areas of the district. About 80 per cent of the villages do not have any medical facility and 48 per cent of the rural population are deprived of it. Villagers have to travel upto 10 kilometres to reach to any medical or health centre. People living in small villages (having the population of less than 1000) suffer the worst because of non-availability of medical amenity.

About 25 per cent villages of the district do not have any educational facility and small villages are the most hard hit among them. Only 18 per cent of the villages are linked by pucca roads and they serve to merely 35 per cent of the village population. Reaching to any medical or health facility, located at a distance, become very difficult if it is not linked by pucca roads. Besides, lack of medical and health facility, 50 per cent of the village population do not have locally available post and telegraph facility while 60 per cent are away from communication facility. Almost 30 per cent village population of the district are deprived of the power supply.

1.3 POVERTY

Eradication of poverty has long been recognised as one of the major challenges confronting human society. The term "poverty" has different meanings for different persons. The methodological and substantial variations in defining and measuring poverty have no limits. The general consensus is that, poverty attains pragmatic and relevant dimensions only within a relative framework. Literature on poverty reveals a variety of perspectives and approaches to the definition and measurement of poverty and implications for policy interventions to eliminate poverty. According to Ravallion, poverty can be said to exist in a given society when individuals/households do not attain a level of material well-being deemed to constitute a reasonable minimum by the standards of that society. Thus, poverty is a phenomenon of relative deprivation where people are regarded as poor if they do not have access to diets, comforts and other entitlements that are customary in that society.

1.3.1 Income Poverty

Income poverty is the poverty defined in terms of income. Poverty is usually thought of as a lack of income-because it is income that is largely assumed to determine one's material standard of well-being. Since there is a functional relationship between income and consumption, reasonably low income always results in low consumption and cosequently in low standard of living. In the Indian context, poverty is measured in terms of poverty line related to income, or more commonly, to estimates of consumption expenditure based on successive rounds of National Sample Survey (NSS). According to official statistics, people whose income is less than the level required to purchase a minimum calorie intake are said to be poor. The concept of income poverty is focused on means rather than ends since the income estimated in terms of money is an approximate way to measure the value of goods and services, that can be purchased out of it.

Chapter 2

METHODOLOGY

OBJECTIVES AND SAMPLING DESIGN

This chapter describes the main objectives and sampling design of the study. To obtain proper and representative sample, a five-stage stratified random sampling model has been used. After highlighting various methodological issues regarding sample selection, the chapter ends with study limitations.

2.1 OBJECTIVES

(a) To assess capability poverty prevalent in Tonk district of Ajmer division in Rajasthan;

(b) To establish relationship between capability poverty and income poverty; and

(c) To suggest measures to eradicate capability poverty.

2.2 SAMPLE DESIGN

The study has adopted multi-stage sampling design in view of the large geographical area involved. Selection of this design was indispensable owing to the need of collecting primary data from wide area, for a given cost. In order to limit the bias in selection and to estimate the sampling error, simple random technique has been used for obtaining the sample. To give proper representation to all types of households living in small and big villages (in terms of population), technique of stratification has been employed to classify all the villages in three strata. In the first four stages there was selection of large primary sampling units with the reduction of sampling frame at each subsequent stage. In the fifth stage, the ultimate sampling units being the households were selected. Multi-stage sampling design proved to be an effective technique for it was easier to administer than most single stage design because of the fact that sampling frame under multi-stage sampling was developed in partial units. Thus, this design facilitated to cover a large area and number of units. The procedure adopted for sampling is as follows:

First stage: In the **first stage**, Ajmer division was selected out of six divisions in Rajasthan namely, Jodhpur, Kota, Udaipur, Jaipur, Ajmer and Bikaner on a random basis.

Second stage: In the **second stage**, Tonk district was selected randomly out of four districts in Ajmer division Viz. Tonk, Bhilwara, Ajmer and Nagaur.

Third stage : Two tehsils namely, Niwai and Tonk out of six tehsils in Tonk district viz. Niwai, Deoli, Malpura, Tonk, Uniara and Todaraisingh, were selected randomly in the **third stage**. The procedure followed for the selection in the next two stages is as under:

Fourth Stage: Selection of Towns and Villages

In this stage, towns and villages were selected from each of the tehsils to give due representation to urban and rural sectors. The technique employed is as follows:

Selection of Towns: As both the tehsils have only one town each, there was no choice involved and both the towns (Niwai and Tonk) were selected to represent urban sector in the sample. To effect reasonably wide coverage, 10 per cent wards from each of the towns were chosen. Thus, 4 out of 35 wards in Tonk town and 2 out of 16 wards in Niwai town were randomly selected in the fourth stage of sampling design.

Selection of Villages: With the object of giving proper representation to different sized villages, all villages of each of the tehsils were classified in the following three strata on the basis of their population.

Stratum I : Villages with population less than 1000.

Stratum II : Villages with population 1000-1999.

Stratum III: Villages with population 2000 and above.

Table 2.1 points out number of villages and households in each stratum.

Table 2.1. Stratum-wise Distribution of Number of Villages and Households in Tonk and Niwai Tehsil

Stratum	Niwai		Tonk	
	Villages	Households	Villages	Households
Stratum I	156	9838	198	12743
Stratum II	19	3454	36	8113
Stratum III	16	6596	14	5591
Total	191	19888	248	26447

Source: Tonk District Census Handbook, 1991.

Table 2.2. Tehsil-wise Selection of Number of Rural and Urban Sample Households

	Niwai			Tonk			All
	Rural	Urban	Total	Rural	Urban	Total	
Households	19888	3731	23619	26447	14620	41067	64686
Sample Households (0.03%)	60	11	71	79	44	123	194

Source: Tonk District Census Handbook, 1991.

To decide the number of households to be selected in the sample, total numbers of rural and urban households for both the tehsils were found out and the sample size was settled at 0.03 per cent of the total number of households in each tehsil. The numbers of rural and urban households in the sample were kept proportionately. Table 2.2 exhibits tehsil-wise selection of rural and urban sample households.

Stratum-wise numbers of rural households and rural sample households for each tehsil are given in Table 2.3.

Table 2.3. Stratum-wise Selection of Number of Rural Households

	Niwai		**Tonk**	
	Households	Sample Households (3 per 1000)	Households	Sample Households (3 per 1000)
Stratum I	9838	30	12743	38
Stratum II	3454	10	8113	24
Stratum III	6596	20	5591	17
Total	19888	60	26447	79

Owing to financial and time constraints it was difficult to contact the households of a large number of villages, belonging to each stratum. Therefore, it was decided to first select certain villages from each of the stratum villages and then choose the households from these selected villages. Stratum-wise classification (Table 2.4) shows that majority of the villages are in stratum I.

In order to keep the number of sample villages limited and to give representation to each stratum, five per cent villages from stratum I and 3 per cent each from stratum II and III were randomly selected. Table 2.4 shows stratum-wise number of sample villages.

Table 2.4 Stratum-wise selection of number of sample villages

	Niwai		Tonk	
	Villages	Sample Villages	Villages	Sample Villages
Stratum I	156	5	198	6
Stratum II	19	1	36	2
Stratum III	16	1	14	1
Total	191	7	248	9

Source: Tonk District Census Handbook, 1991.

Fifth Stage: Selection of Households from Towns and Villages selected in Fourth Stage

Selection of Households from selected Towns: Random selection of 44 households was done from 4 wards in Tonk town, in proportion to the number of households therein. Thus, the formula followed for deciding the number of households to be selected from a ward in Tonk town was as follows:

$$(SH)k = \frac{Hk}{\sum_{k=1}^{l}(H)k} \times (SH)l$$

Where, H = Households; SH = Sample Households;

k = 1,2,..................l wards.

Selection of Households from selected Villages: Random selection of desired number of households from a selected village was done in proportion to number of households in that village to the total number of households in all the selected villages of a particular stratum. Thus, the formula followed was as follows:

$$(SH)ij = \frac{Hij}{(\sum_{i-1}^{n} Hi)j} \times \{(SH)n\}j$$

Where, H = Households; SH = Sample Households;
i = 1, 2,......................n villages;

j = 1,....., m strata.

Figure 1 gives a diagrammatic view of the sampling technique.

2.3 SAMPLE SIZE

Considering the dispersion factor of universe, the desirable level of precision required and the value of additional information against its corresponding cost, an attempt has been made to keep the sample size(n) as optimum as possible. Covering two tehsils of Tonk district in Ajmer division of Rajasthan, the sample consists of 194 households envisaging 1228 individual units. Both rural and urban households have been given proportional representation. The full and diagrammatic view of the sample size is given in figure 2.

2.4 DATA COLLECTION

As the issue is of recent origin, available secondary data at hand are inadequate and therefore it became necessary to largely depend on primary data. In the present study, data have been collected through field survey. Before the main survey, a pilot study was done for testing the schedules and to bring to light their weaknesses and also of the survey techniques. To collect the primary information completely, accurately and to minimise non-response, schedule-cum-observation method has been used. Direct communication with respondents also helped a lot in eliciting information. Application of this method was necessary owing to wide-spread illiteracy particularly among the rural respondents. Primary data included both qualitative and quantitative facts. The investigator along with schedules, went to the respondents and after explaining the aims and objectives of investigation put to them the questions from the proforma in the order the questions were listed and recorded the replies in the space meant for the same in the proforma. The survey period of the study was from May to Nov., 1998. Attempts were made to remove the difficulties that respondents felt in understanding the implications of particular questions or difficult terms. The schedule has been designed to obtain needful information including the size of family, type of house, water and other basic amenities available to the family, literacy status, educational level, food consumption pattern, age distribution of household population, type of attention at birth, antenatal care, etc. Nutritional status of the child has been assessed on the basis of weight for age. The schedule was divided into three sections viz. the household section, the women's section and the children's section. The overall content and format of the schedule have been determined in discussion with the subject experts.

2.5 PROCESSING OF DATA

The relevant data have been processed for making contemplated comparisons and analysis. For processing, the methodology used is as follows:

Editing - raw data have been examined to detect errors and omissions. Consisting of a careful scrutiny of the completed schedules, editing has been done immediately after the interview to ensure that the data are accurate, consistent with other facts gathered, uniformly entered, as complete as possible and have been well arranged to facilitate coding and tabulation.

Coding - was done for efficient analysis and to reduce several responses to a small number of categories. The method of hand coding has been adopted and the data from the schedules have been transcribed to a coding sheet.

Selection Stages	(N) Sampling Frame	Basis	(n) Sample Size
Stage 1 - Divisional Level	6 Division in Rajasthan	Random	1 Ajmer Division
Stage 2 - District Level	4 Districts in Ajmer Division	Random	1 Tonk District
Stage 3 - District Level	6 Tehsil in Tonk District	Random	2 Tehsil viz. Tonk & Niwai
Stage 4 - District Level	Stratum - 1 (Villages having less than 1000 population)	Random (3%)	6 Villages in Tonk t. & 5 Villages in Niwai Tehsil
	Stratum - 2 (Villages having 1000 - 1999 Population)	Random (5%)	2 Villages in Tonk t. & 1 Village in Niwai Tehsil
	Stratum - 3 (Villages having more than 1999 Population)	Random (5%)	1 Village in Tonk t. & 1 Village in Niwai Tehsil
Urban Level	Tonk town - 35 wards	Random (10%)	4 Wards in Tonk town
	Niwai town - 16 wards	Random (10%)	2 Wards in Niwai town
Stage 5 - Househols Level (Rural)	Stratum -1 6 villages in Tonk t. & 5 Villages in Niwai t.	Random	38 Households in Tonk Tehsil & 30 H in Niwai t.
	Stratum - 2 2 Villages in Tonk t. & 1 Village in Niwai t.	Random	24 Households in Tonk Tehsil & 10 H in Niwai t.
Households Level (Urban)	Stratum - 3 1 Village in Tonk t. & 1 Village in Niwai t.	Random	17 Households in Tonk Tehsil & 20 HH in Niwai t.

Note : t = Tehsil; H = Households; tn = Town

Fig. 1. Sampling Techniques: Multi stage Random Sampling

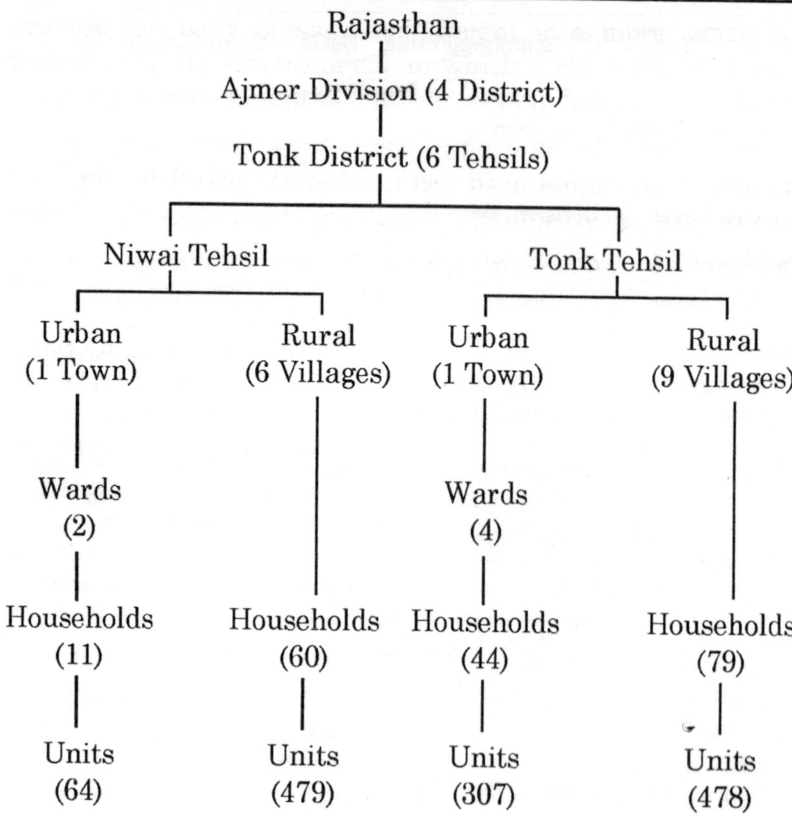

Fig. 2. Sample size

Classification - to derive meaningful relationships, large volumes of raw data have been reduced into homogenous groups and classes. As some of the data as literacy and sex (statistics of attributes) are of descriptive characteristics, their classification has been done according to attributes.

Data relating to age, weight, etc. (statistics of variables) have been classified on the basis of class intervals.

Tabulation - finally, the classified data have been summarised, orderly arranged and displayed through simple and complex tables. Considering the size and type of study and the cost considerations, tabulation has been done manually.

2.6 ANALYSIS OF DATA

Besides tabulation that facilitated to find out the salient features of the data and undertake comparisons, the data have been specifically analysed for drawing inferences about Capability Poverty. The Capability Poverty Measure (CPM) has been worked out to show the percentage of people who lack basic, or minimally essential human capabilities that are needed to lift one from income poverty and to sustain human development. For measuring CPM, the combined index of three critical indicators viz. the proportion of children under five years who are underweight, the proportion of births unattended by trained health personnel and the rate of female illiteracy has been worked out by giving equal weights. In the process of analysis, tests of significance have been applied to set probable limits of constituent variables for the population and find out standard error of the difference between proportions of two samples. Statistical technique of Rank Correlation has been applied to establish the relationship between the capability poverty and the income poverty. To draw statistical inferences, the techniques used are briefed as follows:

(i) Tests of Significance: As the study centres around statistics of attributes, it uses following formulae for tests of significance:

1. Standard error of number of successes: Setting Probable Limits of Constituent variables for the Population

$$PUC/PUB/PIFA \pm 3\ S.E.$$

The standard error is worked out by the following formula:

$$S.E. \text{ of number of successes} = \sqrt{n.p.q}.$$

Where,

S.E. = Standard Error; n = No. of Units in the Sample;

p = Probability of successes (Children being Under weight/ Births being Unattended / Female Adults being Illiterate);

q = Probability of Failures (Children being Normal/ Biths being Attended by Trained Health Personnel / Female Adults being Literate);

PUC = The Proportion of Underweight Children;

PUB = The Proportion of Unattended Births; and

PIFA = The Proportion of Illiterate Female Adults.

2. Standard Error of the Difference between Proportions of Two Samples

To find out whether-

(i) the difference between rural and urban sample is significant or not;

(ii) the difference between two tehsils is significant or not; and

(iii) the difference between male and female is significant or not.

The standard error of the difference between proportions of two samples is worked out by applying the following formula:

$$S.E.\,\text{Diff}.\text{P1} - \text{P2}\sqrt{p\,q(\frac{1}{n_1}+\frac{1}{n_2})}$$

Where,

p = Best estimate of proportion in the population and is obtained as follows:

$$p = \frac{n_1 p_1 + n_2 p_2}{n_1 + n_2}$$

q = 1-(p);

n_1 = Number of events in sample No. one.

n_2 = Number of events in sample No. two.

(ii) Correlation : To establish statistical relationship between income and capability, following correlation methods are applied:

1. Rank Correlation between Capability Poverty Measure Rank and Real GDP Per Capita (PPP$) Rank

$$p = 1 - \frac{6\sum d^2}{n(n^2 - 1)}$$

Where,

p = Spearman's rank correlation coefficient;

d = Difference of ranks;

n = Number of ranks.

2. Coefficient of Correlation by Karl Pearson's Method

$$r = \frac{\sum XY - n\overline{X}\,\overline{Y}}{\sqrt{\sum X^2 - n\overline{X}^2}\ \sqrt{\sum Y^2 - n\overline{Y}^2}}$$

Probable Error (P.E.) of the Coefficient of Correlation

$$P.E. = 0.6745\frac{1 - r^2}{\sqrt{n}}$$

(iii) Capability Poverty Measure

To assess capability poverty, an index known as capability poverty measure has been worked out. This measure is an average of the following three variables:

$$CPM = \frac{PUC + PUB + PIFA}{3}$$

Where,

CPM = Capability Poverty Measure;

PUC = The Proportion of Underweight Children;

PUB = The Proportion of Unattended Births; and

PIFA = The Proportion of Illiterate Female Adults.

1. The percentage of children under five who are underweight (PUC) =

$$\frac{\text{No. of Underweight Children}}{\text{Total No. of Children}} \times 100$$

or $$PUC = \frac{\sum_{a=0}^{60} UCa}{\sum_{a=0}^{60} Ca} \times 100$$

Where,

UC = No. of Underweight Children.

C = No. of Children.

a = 0,1,2,...60 months.

2. The percentage of births unattended by trained health personnel (PUB) =

$$\frac{\text{No. of Unattended Births}}{\text{Total No. of Births}} \times 100$$

or $$PUB = \frac{\sum_{a=0}^{N} UBa}{\sum_{a=0}^{N} Ba} \times 100$$

Where, UB = No. of Unattended Births.

B = No. of Births.

a = 0,1,2,..................60 months.

3. The percentage of women aged 15 years and above who are illiterate (PIFA) =

$$\frac{\text{No. of Illiterate Female Adults}}{\text{Total No. of Female Adults}} \times 100$$

or $$PIFA = \frac{\sum_{w=15}^{55+} IFAw}{\sum_{w=15}^{55+} FAw} \times 100$$

Where,

IFA = No. of Illiterate Female Adults.

FA = No. of Female Adults.

w = 15, 16,....................................55 years.

To facilitate analysis, sampling units are classified (Table 2.5) in different constituents.

Table 2.5. Sample Constituents

Particulars	Niwai			Tonk			
	Urban	Rural	Total	Urban	Rural	Total	All
Male	**34**	**201**	**235**	**159**	**248**	**407**	**642**
(i) Under-5 Children	6	31	37	25	43	68	105
(ii) Others	28	170	198	134	205	339	537
Female	**30**	**178**	**208**	**148**	**230**	**378**	**586**
(i) Under-5 Children	4	31	35	24	38	62	97
(ii) 15+ Adults	17	106	123	86	138	224	347
(iii) others	9	41	50	38	54	92	142
Total	**64**	**379**	**443**	**307**	**478**	**785**	**1228**

2.7 CONCEPTS AND DEFINITIONS

Births Attended - The percentage of births attended by physicians, nurses, midwives, trained primary health care workers or trained traditional birth attendants.

Daily Calorie Requirement Per Capita - The average number of calories needed to sustain a person at normal levels of activity and health, taking into account the distribution of the population by age, sex, bodyweight and environmental temperature.

Dependency Ratio - The ratio of the population defined as dependent-those under 15 and those over 64-to the working-age population, aged between 15 and 64.

Doctors - Refers to physicians and includes all graduates of any faculty or school of medicine in any medical field (including practice, teaching, administration and research).

Enrollment Ratio (Gross and Net) -The gross enrollment ratio is the number of students enrolled in a level of education, whether or not they belong in the relevant age group for that level, as a percentage of the population in the relevant age group for that level. The net enrollment ratio is the number of students enrolled in a level of education who belong in the relevant age group, as part of the population in that group.

Health Services Access - The percentage of the population that can reach appropriate local health services on foot or by means of transport in no more than one hour.

Household - A household is a group of persons who commonly live together and would take their meals from a common kitchen unless the exigencies of work prevent any of them from doing so. There may be one member households, two member households or multi-member households. The important link in finding out whether there is a household or not is a common kitchen.

Human Priority Areas - Basic education, primary health care, safe drinking water, adequate sanitation, family planning and nutrition.

Human Development Index (HDI) - A composite measure of human development containing indicators representing three equally weighted dimensions of human development - longevity (life expectancy at birth), Knowledge (adult literacy and mean years of schooling), and income (purchasing power parity dollars per capita).

Immunized - The average vaccination coverage of children under one year of age for antigenused in the Universal Child Immunization (UCI) Programme.

Infant Mortality Rate - The annual number of deaths of infants under one year of age per 1000 live births. More specifically, the probability of dying between birth and exactly one year of age.

Life Expectancy at Birth - The number of years a new born infant would live if prevailing patterns of mortality at the time of birth were to stay the same throughout the child's life.

Literacy Rate (adult) - The percentage of people aged 15 and above who can, with understanding, both read and write a short, simple statement on their everyday life.

Literate - A person is considered to be literate if he/she is able to both read and write with understanding in any language. A person who can merely read but cannot write, is not literate. It is not necessary that a person who is literate should have passed any minimum educational standard. However, all children of the age of 6 years or less are treated as illiterate even if the child is going to a school and may have picked up reading and writing a few words.

Low-Birth-Weight Infants - The percentage of babies born weighing less than 2,500 grams.

Mean Years of Schooling - Average number of years of schooling received per person age 25 and above.

Maternal Mortality Rate - The annual number of deaths of women from pregnancy-related causes per 1,00,000 live births.

Nurses - All persons who have completed a programme of basic nursing education and are qualified and registered or authorised by the country to provide responsible and competent service for the promotion of health, prevention of illness, care of sick and rehabilitation.

Primary Education - Education at the first level (International Standard Classification of Education[ISCED] level 1), the main function of which is to provide the basic elements of education, such as elementary schools and primary schools.

Primary School Completion Rate - The proportion of the children entering the first grade of primary school who successfully complete that level in due course.

Nutritional Status (Reference Standard) - A reference standard can be defined as "that coveted nutritional status in which a person suffers from no disability in any of his nutrition-related functions (such as immunological competence, physical work capacity, cognitive function, reproductive capacity etc.)".

Rural Urban Disparity - A set of national, regional and other estimates in which all the rural figures are expressed in relation to the corresponding urban figures, which are indexed to equal 100.

Rural /Urban Population - The percentage of the population living in rural/urban areas as defined according to the national definition used in the most recent population census.

Safe Water Access - The percentage of the population with reasonable access to safe water supply, including treated safe waters or untreated but uncontaminated water such as those from springs sanitary wells and protected boreholes.

Sanitation Access - The percentage of the population with access to sanitary means of excreta and waste disposal, including outdoor latrines and composting.

Stunting - The percentage of children, between 24 and 59 months, below minus two standard deviations from the median height-for-age of the reference population.

Wasting - The percentage of children, between 12 and 23 months, below minus two standard deviations from the median weight-for-height of the reference population.

Under-five Mortality Rate - The annual number of deaths of children under five years of age per 1,000 live births. More specifically, the probability of dying between birth and exactly five years of age.

Underweight (moderate and severe child malnutrition) - The percentage of children under age five who are below minus two standard deviations from the median birth-weight -for-age of the reference population.

Working Mother - A mother who is away from home for 6 hours or more at a stretch is defined as a working mother.

2.8 LIMITATIONS

1. To assess capability poverty, this study has employed 'Capability Poverty Measure' as an index which takes into accont only three critically essential human capabilities. Therefore, the numerical value of CPM is meaningful only in the relative framework. This measure commands properties of comparison only to the extent of its chosen indicators and thus it is not a perfect measuring rod applicable in all stages of develop-

ment. Adult Female Literacy, for example, may be a good indicator in developing countries, but it does not help to provide a ranking in say, the countries of Western Europe, all of which have 100 per cent literacy. Thus, a country with very low CPM value does not mean that it is absolutely well off in all respects. It also does not automatically mean that the population has all the required capabilities to take advantage of the available opportunities. There is scope for constructive dissent and fruitful debate over the use of this measure.

2. This study does not take into account other human deprivations that also affect the capability status of individuals.
3. In this study, all the three variables have been given equal weight. Thus, results may vary if unequal weights are assigned to the variables.

Notes

The population figures of villages and towns have been drawn from the District Census Handbook, 1991.

Chapter 3

RESULTS – 1

UNDERWEIGHT CHILDREN AND THEIR DETERMINANTS

The analysis is based on primary and secondary data pertaining to children being underweight; adult females being illiterate and births being unattended. Since income data from primary sources have not been collected, it is not possible to workout area specific correlations between income and capability. Alternatively, attempt has been made to establish the relationship between income and capability from data available of different selected countries. The study presents the results in five sections. First three sections deal with analysis and measurement of underweight children, unattended births and female illiteracy. Section 4 takes up computation of capability poverty measure. Last section attempts to establish the relationship between income and capability. Results are based on quantitative as well as qualitative data gathered through a field survey.

1. Underweight Children

The proportion of underweight children is a powerful variable in the assessment of the capability poverty. It reflects lack of opportunity in a number of areas, most important among them are:

1. Nutrition;

2. Health Services;
3. Safe water; and
4. Sanitation.

In a human life, pre-school age is the period when growth is the most rapid. During this phase the human growth appears to be particularly sensitive to outside influences both at the household level and the environment level: like the adequacy of nutrition and the state of hygiene, care and attention received, type of water supply, immunisation, environmental infections and even child abuse. It is, perhaps, the most vulnerable period and sustained deprivations experienced then, resulting in growth impairment, can lead to permanent stunting (lower heights) of those individuals as adults. Removal of deprivations at older ages does not result in 'catch-up growth' later. Thus, childhood is a particularly interesting period for studying body-size variations.

Nutrition is a basic necessity for individual's health and capability development. It is considered as one of the most important factors responsible for proper growth in infancy and childhood. Undernutrition being a reflection of unfulfilled dietary demands, is most likely to occur during the three most demanding periods in human life: (i) *growing age- infants and children;* (ii) *pregnancy*; and (iii) *the period of lactation- nursing women*. Malnutrition during the critical phases of early growth can lead not only to the stunting of physical growth but also to suboptimal intellectual development and poor neurointegrative competence in children. Undernutrition in pregnancy leaves its scars even on the foetus and results in the birth of low weight babies. Similarly, the period of lactation is crucially important not only for nursing mothers but also to their babies. Mothers' nutritional deficiency in this period often hit their babies badly. Evidence shows that there is a statistical relationship between 'diet adequacy' and 'weight and height.' Inadequate diets result in retarded weight and height.

Types of Malnutrition: The dictionary meaning of malnutrition is 'imperfect or faulty nutrition.' It can be simply defined as a precipitated (or even latent) stage of disproportion between demands of the body for a certain nutrient and its intake. Logically, therefore, there could be two types of malnutrition; one in which the demand is not fully met, and the other when the nutrient is consumed in excess. The first condition is undernutrition and the second overnutrition. In India undernutrition is more prevalent and it is only in rare situations that overnutrition exists. In general usage, therefore, the terms malnutrition and undernutrition have come to be taken as almost synonymous.

Besides nutrients, the availability of safe water and good sanitary conditions is important for the child growth. Unfortunately, the proportions of 'safe water access' and 'sanitary access' are miserably low in many countries. Unsafe water supply and unhealthy sanitary conditions recurrently generate vicious circles of diseases and result in the low weight of the suffering children. Millions of children die every year due to diarhhoea and other water and sanitary related diseases and those who survive lose their weights significantly. The problem takes alarming proportions particularly when the health services are not available.

The nutritional status of individuals can be assessed either by (i) input or food adequacy criteria of estimated per capita calorie and protein intakes or by (ii) output criteria of physical assessments of height and weight-the anthropometric measures. The latter criterion is specifically used for assessing the nutritional status of children under five years of age.

1.1 Anthropometric Measures

Anthropometric data have been repeatedly used for comparisons between population groups and individuals, and to make inferences about the health, mortality levels, the environment and general standards of living. Among economic historians and those who study historical demography as well, there is an increasing interest in exploring anthropometric measurements and understanding their relationship to living standards. In recent years economists have employed weight and height data to draw inferences about health, nutrition and, hence, aspects of welfare.

Systematic differences in body sizes of individuals are recognised as reflecting their different health and nutritional status, especially after controlling for genetic factors. Data on children's heights and weights can serve as indicators of aspects of well-being and of socio-economic inequality within and between population groups. Such data permit comparisons at a time as well as over time. In anthropometric measures, the nutritional status of children is measured by using the following three summary indices:

(I) Weight-for-age;

(II) Height-for-age; and

(III) Weight-for-height

These measures are useful in assessing the children's growth, their susceptibility to diseases and chances of survival. Each of the indices provides somewhat different information about nutritional status.

The **height-for-age** index measures linear growth retardation among children. Children who are more than two standard deviations below the median of the reference population, for height-for-age are considered short for their age or *stunted.* The percentage in this category indicates the prevalence of chronic undernutrition which often leads to chronic or recurrent diarrhoea. Stunting is typically associated with inadequate food intake resulting from poor feeding practices or from the lack of sufficient food, as well as the existence of adverse environmental conditions for an extended period of time. Moderate and severe undernutrition can be ascertained for a child of a given age and sex by comparing the recorded observation on height (in cms) with that of the median for the reference population. Height-for-age, therefore, is a measure of the long-term effects of undernutrition.

The **weight-for-height** index measures body mass in relation to body length. Gender-specific and age-independent norms are available on median weights for given heights. If the recorded weight for a given height is less than two standard deviations (or 80 per cent) of the median weight value of the reference population, the child is identified as moderately undernourished, too thin or *wasted.* The percentage in this category indicates the prevalence of acute undernutrition. This condition is associated with the failure to receive adequate nutrition in the period immediately before the survey and may be the result of seasonal variations in food supply or recent episodes of illness (especially diarrhoea). It may be added that a child classified as undernourished using both weight-for-age and height-for age indices may not be classified as undernourished in terms of the weight-for-height indicator due to the process of 'adaption'.

The **Weight-for-age** is a composite measure that takes into account both chronic and acute undernutrition. Children who are more than two standard deviations below the reference median on this index are considered *under weight.* A child of a given age (in months) and sex is said to be moderately undernourished when his or her weight (in kgs) falls below two standard deviations of the median of the reference population, and severely undernourished, when his or her weight falls below three standard deviations of the median. With stress, weights normally are first affected, but height, growth and change in other anthropometric indicators soon follow. Similarly, if the danger recedes, weight, height and other signs of growth return. Weight is a measure of body mass. It automatically takes into account height to a certain extent since the taller a person is, the greater the body mass. Thus, weight is a more sensitive indicator to the environment in which a child grows in the short run, while height is a longer term indicator.

In the present study, weight-for-age indicator (proportion of underweight children) has been employed as one of the three constituent variables of CPM for the assessment of capability deprivation. As an outcome variable, it registers the effect of many input variables.

1.2 Indian Profile

Children between the ages of one and five years constitute more than 15 per cent of our population and they are the most vulnerable to malnutrition. It is well known that a very large proportion of our children belonging to low income groups are severely undernourished. In India, 53 per cent of the children (under age five) are underweight, in spite of the improvement in the consumption levels of both energy and protein between 1975 and 1989. Regarding severe malnutrition, however a noticeable decline has been observed in most states. But actual levels are still high in some states. The proportion of underweight children under age five has reduced from 71 per cent in 1975 to 53 in 1990-97. The severest effect of malnutrition results in a very high infant mortality. In the country as a whole, in 1990, 125 children out of 1000 live births died before their fifth birthday. There is wide inter-state disparity in the under-five (U-5) mortality levels. While in Kerala the U-5 mortality rate in 1990 was 27 per 1000, it was 157 in Rajasthan, 162 in Uttar Pradesh and 185 in Madhya Pradesh. The U-5 mortality rate for females is higher than that for males in most of the larger states except Andhra Pradesh, Karnataka, Kerala, Maharashtra and Tamil Nadu. The U-5 mortality rate gap between male and female in 1990 is very high in the states of Uttar Pradesh (180/145), Rajasthan (172/144), Madhya Pradesh (194/177), and Bihar (140/117). For the country as a whole, the U-5 mortality in rural areas in 1990 was 137 compared to 76 in urban areas. In rural areas, the rate varies from a very high level of 200 in Madhya Pradesh to 172 in Uttar Pradesh, 167 in Rajasthan and only 27 in Kerala. The U-5 mortality rate in Rajasthan (urban) is 99.

1.3 Study Results

Displaying distribution of children by age, sex and residence, Table 3.1 shows that the sample consisted of 143 rural and 59 urban children. Among the rural children there were 74 males and 69 females while urban children included 31 males and 28 females. Classification by age in months points out varying number of children in each class. In 31-36 months' age class there were 27 children as compared to 15 in 55-60 months' class.

Table 3.1. Distribution of Children by Age, Sex and Residence

	Rural			Urban			Total		No. of Children (Total)
	M	F	T	M	F	T	M	F	
0-6	9	8	17	5	2	7	14	10	24
7-12	6	8	14	3	4	7	9	12	21
13-18	5	7	12	3	2	5	8	9	17
19-24	8	6	14	1	1	2	9	7	16
25-30	5	8	13	5	3	8	10	11	21
31-36	12	8	20	3	4	7	15	12	27
37-42	6	7	13	5	4	9	11	11	22
43-46	9	7	16	0	3	3	9	10	19
47-54	9	7	16	2	2	4	11	9	20
55-60	5	3	8	4	3	7	9	6	15
Total	74	69	143	31	28	59	105	97	202

Out of 202 children, 130 were selected from Tonk tehsil and 72 from Niwai tehsil. Children from Tonk tehsil consisted of 81 rural and 49 urban. While among 72 Niwai tehsil children, 62 were rural and 10 urban. Results based on weight-for-age indicate that out of 105 boys, there were 49 normal as compared to 56 underweight (Table 3.2, Figure 3). Among 97 girls, 42 were found normal and 55 underweight. Tehsil-wise data reflect that in Niwai, out of 35 girls only 11 were weighed as normal in comparison to 24 underweight. However, in Tonk tehsil, numbers of under-weight and normal girls were found exactly equal. In all, underweight children (111) were proportionately more than the normal ones (91). Rural children included 60 normal and 83 underweight while urban contained 31 normal and 28 under weight children. The proportion of underweight children was more in rural areas as compared to that in urban areas. Proportion of underweight children was found more in Niwai tehsil as compared to that in Tonk tehsil.

Table 3.2. Distribution of Children by Sex, Residence and Extent of Malnutrition

Particulars	Tonk Tehsil			Niwai Tehsil			Total		
	Rural	Urban	Total	Rural	Urban	Total	Rural	Urban	Total
Males	43	25	68	31	6	37	74	31	105
Normal	19	12	31	14	4	18	33	16	49
Underweight	24	13	37	17	2	19	41	15	56
Females	38	24	62	31	4	35	69	28	97
Normal	18	13	31	9	2	11	27	15	42
Underweight	20	11	31	22	2	24	42	13	55
Total	81	49	130	62	10	72	143	59	202
Normal	37	25	62	23	6	29	60	31	91
Underweight	44	24	68	39	4	43	83	28	111

Source: Field Survey.

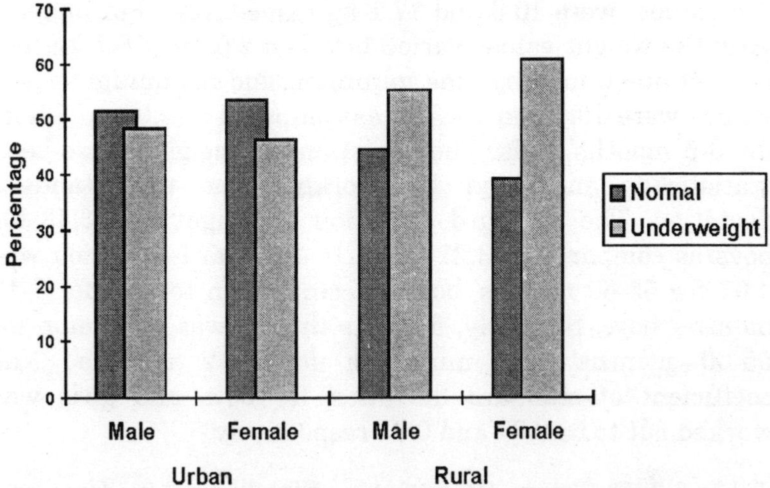

Fig. 3. Distribution of Children by Sex, Residence and Extent of Malnutrition

Manifesting the statistics on average weight of children of less than five years of age, Table 3.3 shows that average weight of boys was 10.39 kg and of girls 9.78 kg. It was found that average weight increased with each subsequent age group indicating that it is the period when weight and height increase very fast. The average weight was 14.0 kg for 55-60 months' age as compared to 5.06 kg for 0-6 months' age.

There have been considerable variations in the weights of children of each age group reflecting the chances of being underweight. Further, it is worth noting that each class is made of 6 months and the weight of a lesser age child is bound to be less than a child of higher age in the same class and thus resulting in big gap in the minimum and maximum weight of that class. However, malnourishment has contributed significantly in the enlargement of this gap. For under 5 boys the minimum and maximum values for weight were 1.8 and 17.1 kg respectively. While the minimum and maximum values for 0-6 months' class males were 1.8 and 8.2 kg respectively, for 55-60 months' class the values were 10.6 and 17.1 kg respectively. For under 5 girls the weight values varied between 2.0 and 16.7 kg. For girls of 55-60 months', the minimum and maximum weight values were 10.7 and 16.7 kg as compared to 2.0 and 7.5 kg for 0-6 months' girls. The variations in weights have been statistically measured by working out the standard deviation. The standard deviation of weight was 3.43 for boys as compared to 3.21 for girls. Standard deviation was 2.61 for 55-60 months' boys in comparison to 1.21 for 7-12 months' boys. Similarly, for girls the SD was maximum for 55-60 months' and minimum for 7-12 months'. The coefficient of standard deviation for boys and girls was worked out to be 0.37 and 0.33 respectively.

Table 3.3. Summary Statistics on Weight by Age, Boys and Girls

Age (in months)	Boys						Girls					
	N	AM	SD	Min	Max	CSD	N	AM	SD	Min	Max	CSD
0-6	14	5.06	1.97	1.8	8.2	0.39	10	4.55	1.61	2.0	7.5	0.35
7-12	9	7.78	1.21	6.1	9.7	0.16	12	6.93	1.28	5.4	9.1	0.18
13-18	8	9.05	2.08	6.5	11.9	0.23	9	7.92	1.47	6.2	10.1	0.19
19-24	9	9.13	1.55	7.2	11.5	0.17	7	8.71	1.75	6.8	11.2	0.20
25-30	10	10.33	1.73	7.6	12.7	0.17	11	9.76	1.53	7.4	12.5	0.16
31-36	15	11.17	2.11	7.4	15.6	0.19	12	10.73	1.77	8.5	13.1	0.16
37-42	11	12.25	2.41	8.6	16.1	0.20	11	11.62	2.13	8.3	15.3	0.18
43-48	9	12.41	2.03	9.2	14.7	0.16	10	12.44	2.07	10.2	15.8	0.17
49-54	11	14.02	2.09	10.7	16.5	0.15	9	12.66	2.02	9.7	14.9	0.14
55-60	9	14.00	2.61	10.6	17.1	0.19	6	14.02	2.33	10.7	16.7	0.17
All	105	10.39	3.43	1.8	17.1	0.33	97	9.77	3.21	2.0	16.7	0.33

Source: Field Survey.

Notes : Weight is measured in kgs.

N: Number of observations; AM: Arithmetic Mean; SD: Standard; Deviation; Min: Minimum Value; Max: Maximum Value; CSD: Coefficient of Standard Deviation.

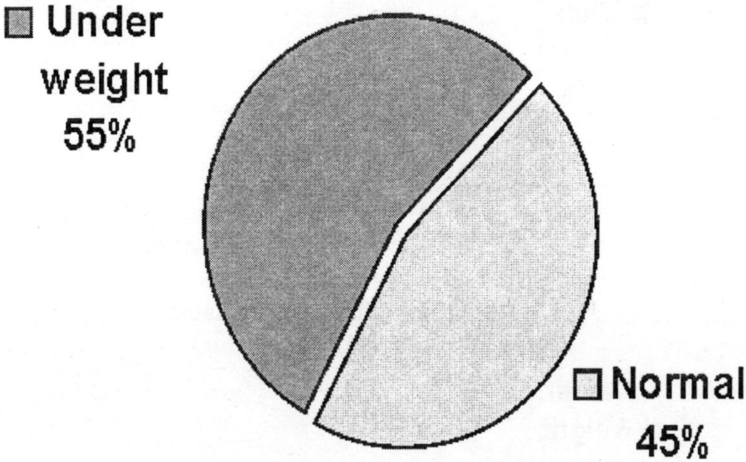

Fig. 4. Nutritional Status of Children
(Using Weight for Age Indicator)

In percentage terms, 55 per cent children were found underweight in comparison to 45 per cent normal (Table 3.4, Figure 4). The percentage of underweight children was minimum (37.5%) in the 0-6 months' age group of children and increased to 47.6 per cent in the 7-12 months' age group. In the children above 1 year of age, the proportion of underweight children always remained more than 50% and it was even more than 60% in the 19-36 months' age classes. In the age-group of 19-24 months, 68.7 per cent children were noticed as underweight. Sex-wise data (Fig. 5, 6) reflect that the percentage of underweight females (56.7%) was slightly more than that of underweight males (53.3%). However, this does not mean that in each age group, more females were malnourished. Malnutrition was more prevalent in females in some age groups while in others it was the reverse.

Fig. 5. Nutritional Status of Females
(Using Weight for Age Indicator)

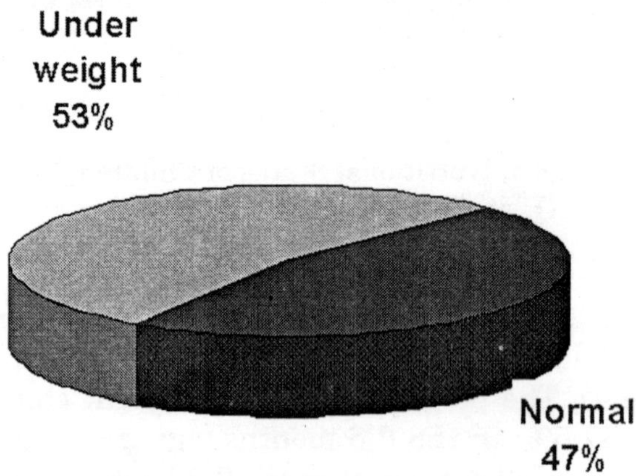

Fig. 6. Nutritional Status of Males
(Using Weight for Age Indicator)

It has been observed that nutritional condition of children living in very small villages is considerably worse. Reasons are not difficult to find as most of the villages do not have any health facility. Poor and uncertain income resources, lack of awareness, low literacy, superstitious beliefs, etc. work as major retardants. About 70 per cent of the under five children living in stratum I villages (Fig. 7) are underweight. In stratum I villages only 30.6 per cent children were weighed as normal and 69.4 per cent children were found underweight (Table 3.5). The dismal fact is that among the underweight children 50 per cent children were severely underweight. Considering weight for age indicator, the nutritional status of children of II and III strata villages is comparatively better. In stratum II and III villages more than 50 per cent of the children were found normal and proportion of severely underweight children was less than that of moderately underweight children. Among the underweight children, 44 were moderately underweight and 39 severely underweight. What is more worrisome is that in some age groups viz. 7-12, 19-24, 25-30 months, more than 80 per cent of stratum I children are nutritionally poor and underweight (Table 3.6). In all, out of 143 rural children, 60 (41.9%) were normal and 83 (58.1%) underweight. Among the underweight children, 44 were moderately underweight and 39 severely underweight.

Table 3.4. Nutritional Status of Children

Age of Child (in Mon-ths)	Males						Females						Total					
	Normal		Under eight		Total		Normal		Under eight		Total		Normal		Under weight		Total	
	N	%	N	%	N	%	N	%	N	%	N	%	N	%	N	%	N	%
0-6	9	(64.3)	5	(35.7)	14	(100.0)	6	(60.0)	4	(40.0)	10	(100.0)	15	(62.5)	9	(37.5)	24	(100.0)
7-12	5	(55.6)	4	(44.4)	9	(100.0)	6	(50.0)	6	(50.0)	12	(100.0)	11	(52.4)	10	(47.6)	21	(100.0)
13-18	4	(50.0)	4	(50.0)	8	(100.0)	4	(44.4)	5	(55.6)	9	(100.0)	8	(47.1)	9	(52.9)	17	(100.0)
19-24	3	(33.3)	6	(66.7)	9	(100.0)	2	(28.6)	5	(71.4)	7	(100.0)	5	(31.3)	11	(68.7)	16	(100.0)
25-30	4	(40.0)	6	(60.0)	10	(100.0)	4	(36.4)	7	(63.6)	11	(100.0)	8	(38.1)	13	(61.9)	21	(100.0)
31-36	6	(40.0)	9	(60.0)	15	(100.0)	4	(33.3)	8	(66.7)	12	(100.0)	10	(37.0)	17	(63.0)	27	(100.0)
37-42	5	(45.5)	6	(54.5)	11	(100.0)	5	(45.5)	6	(54.5)	11	(100.0)	10	(45.5)	12	(54.5)	22	(100.0)
43-48	4	(44.4)	5	(55.6)	9	(100.0)	4	(40.0)	6	(60.0)	10	(100.0)	8	(42.1)	11	(57.9)	19	(100.0)
49-54	5	(45.5)	6	(54.5)	11	(100.0)	4	(44.4)	5	(55.5)	9	(100.0)	9	(45.0)	11	(55.0)	20	(100.0)
55-60	4	(44.4)	5	(55.6)	9	(100.0)	3	(50.0)	3	(50.0)	6	(100.0)	7	(46.7)	8	(53.3)	15	(100.0)
All	49	(46.7)	56	(53.3)	105	(100.0)	42	(43.3)	55	(56.7)	97	(100.0)	91	(45.0)	111	(55.0)	202	(100.0)

Source: Field Survey.

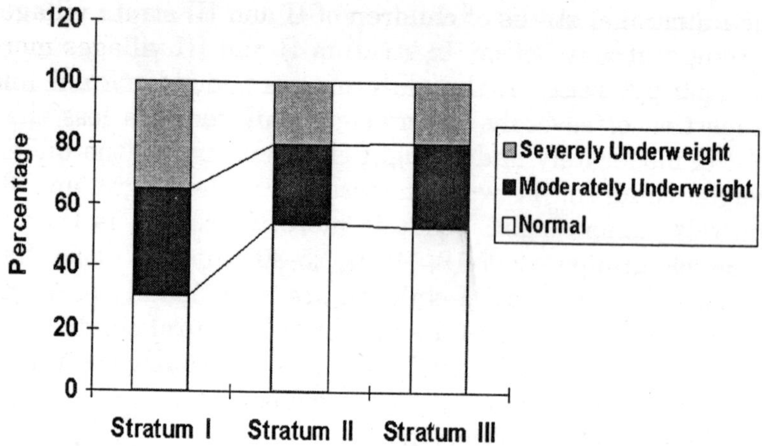

Fig. 7. Distributional of Rural Children by Stratum and Degree of Malnutrition

Table 3.5. Stratum-wise Distribution of Rural Children According to Degree of Malnutrition

Degree of Malnutrition	Stratum I		Stratum II		Stratum III		Total	
	N	(%)	N	(%)	N	(%)	N	(%)
Normal	22	30.6	19	54.3	19	52.8	60	41.9
Moderately Underweight	25	34.7	9	25.7	10	27.8	44	30.8
Severely Underweight	25	34.7	7	20.0	7	19.4	39	27.3
Total	72	100.0	35	100.0	36	100.0	143	100.0

Source: Field Survey

Moderately Underweight: A child is moderately underweight if its weight is less than 'median-2 SD' but more than 'median- 3 SD.'

Severely Underweight: A child is severely underweight if its weight is less than 'median-3 SD.'

Table 3.6. Stratum-wise Distribution of Underweight Children in Rural Areas

Age in Child (in months)	Stratum I			Stratum II			Stratum III			Total		
	N	U	T	N	U	T	N	U	T	N	U	T
0-6	4	6	10	2	1	3	3	1	4	9	8	17
	(40.0)	(60.0)	(100.0)	(66.7)	(33.3)	(100.0)	(75.0)	(25.0)	(100.0)	(52.9)	(47.1)	(100)
7-12	1	7	8	3	1	4	2	0	2	6	8	14
	(12.5)	(87.5)	(100.0)	(75.0)	(25.0)	(100.0)	(100.0)	(0.0)	(100.0)	(42.9)	(57.1)	(100)
13-18	3	2	5	1	3	4	1	2	3	5	7	12
	(60.0)	(40.0)	(100.0)	(25.0)	(75.0)	(100.0)	(33.3)	(66.7)	(100.0)	(41.7)	(58.3)	(100)
19-24	1	5	6	3	2	5	1	2	3	5	9	14
	(16.7)	(83.3)	(100.0)	(60.0)	(40.0)	(100.0)	(33.3)	(66.7)	(100.0)	(35.7)	(64.3)	(100)
25-30	1	6	7	2	1	3	2	1	3	5	8	13
	(16.7)	(83.3)	(100.0)	(66.7)	(33.3)	(100.0)	(66.7)	(33.3)	(100.0)	(38.5)	(61.5)	(100)
31-36	3	7	10	2	4	6	2	2	4	7	13	20
	(30.0)	(70.0)	(100.0)	(33.3)	(66.7)	(100.0)	(50.0)	(50.0)	(100.0)	(35.0)	(65.0)	(100)
37-42	2	5	7	2	0	2	2	2	4	6	7	13
	(28.6)	(71.4)	(100.0)	(100.0)	(0.0)	(100.0)	(50.0)	(50.0)	(100.0)	(37.5)	(62.5)	(100)
43-48	3	5	8	2	2	4	2	2	4	7	9	16
	(37.5)	(62.5)	(100.0)	(50.0)	(50.0)	(100.0)	(50.0)	(50.0)	(100.0)	(43.8)	(56.2)	(100)
49-54	2	5	7	2	1	3	3	3	6	7	9	16
	(28.6)	(71.4)	(100.0)	(66.7)	(33.3)	(100.0)	(50.0)	(50.0)	(100.0)	(43.8)	(56.2)	(100)
55-60	2	2	4	0	1	1	1	2	3	3	5	8
	(50.0)	(50.0)	(100.0)	(0.0)	(100.0)	(100.0)	(33.3)	(66.7)	(100.0)	(37.5)	(62.5)	(100)
All	22	50	72	19	16	35	19	17	36	60	83	143
	(30.6)	(69.4)	(100.0)	(54.3)	(45.7)	(100.0)	(52.8)	(47.2)	(100.0)	(42.0)	(58.0)	(100)

N = Normal; U = Underweight; T = Total

Among the under 5 boys, 46.7 per cent were assessed as normal and 53.3 per cent underweight. Underweight consisted of 30.5 per cent moderately underweight and 22.8 per cent severely underweight. Upto 12 months' age, majority of the children were normal and almost all the underweight children were moderately underweight. But thereafter the percentage of underweight children increased with varying percentage of severely underweight children. Table 3.7 shows that in the age group of 13-18, 19-24, 55-60, the percentage of severely underweight was more than the moderately underweight children.

Table 3.7. Prevalence of Undernutrition among Boys

Age (in months)	Normal		Underweight						All	
			Moderate		Severe		Total			
	N	%	N	%	N	%	N	%	N	%
0-6	9	64.3	4	28.6	1	7.1	5	35.7	14	100.0
7-12	5	55.6	4	44.4	0	0.0	4	44.4	9	100.0
13-18	4	50.0	1	12.5	3	37.5	4	50.0	8	100.0
19-24	3	33.3	2	22.2	4	44.5	6	66.7	9	100.0
25-30	4	40.0	3	30.0	3	30.0	6	60.0	10	100.0
31-36	6	40.0	5	33.3	4	26.7	9	60.0	15	100.0
37-42	5	45.5	4	36.4	2	18.1	6	54.5	11	100.0
43-48	4	44.4	3	33.3	2	22.3	5	55.6	9	100.0
49-54	5	45.5	4	36.4	2	18.1	6	54.5	11	100.0
55-60	4	44.5	2	22.2	3	33.3	5	55.5	9	100.0
All	49	46.7	32	30.5	24	22.8	56	53.3	105	100.0

Source: Field Survey.

Among the under 5 girls, 43.3 per cent were found normal and 56.7 per cent underweight. A disturbing fact is that severely underweight girls are proportionately more than those of the moderately underweight. Table 3.8 shows that amid the female children of more than 6 months of age, percentage of malnourished children remained varying between 50 and 70 touching the high of 71.4 in the 19-24 age group. Birth order of the children and severity of malnutrition was also found to be associated. Children having first or second birth order had lower prevalence of malnutrition than those who had a birth order of more than three. The low prevalence of malnutrition in children having first or second birth order may be because smaller the number of children in a family; the more attention and care is exercised.

Table 3.8. Prevalence of Undernutrition among Girls

Age (in months)	Normal		Underweight						All	
			Moderate		Severe		Total			
	N	(%)	N	(%)	N	(%)	N	(%)	N	(%)
0-6	6	60.0	3	30.0	1	10.0	4	40.0	10	100.0
7-12	6	50.0	3	25	3	25	6	50.0	12	100.0
13-18	4	44.4	1	11.2	4	44.4	5	55.6	9	100.0
19-24	2	28.6	2	28.6	3	42.8	5	71.4	7	100.0
25-30	4	36.4	4	36.4	3	27.2	7	63.6	11	100.0
31-36	4	33.3	4	33.3	4	33.3	8	66.7	12	100.0
37-42	5	45.5	3	27.2	3	27.3	6	54.5	11	100.0
43-48	4	40.0	3	30.0	3	30.0	6	60.0	10	100.0
49-54	4	44.5	2	22.2	3	33.3	5	55.5	9	100.0
55-60	3	50.0	2	33.3	1	16.7	3	50.0	6	100.0
All	42	43.3	27	27.8	28	28.9	55	56.7	97	100.0

Exhibiting the stratum-wise distribution of rural underweight children, Table 3.9 points out that proportion of underweight children is the highest in stratum I villages.

It underscores the necessity for provision of health, education, drinking water and other amenities in these areas to improve peoples' accessibility. The nutritional status of children is comparatively better in villages of II and III strata. The proportion of underweight children in stratum I villages of Niwai tehsil is 76.7 as compared to 64.3 per cent in Tonk tehsil. Regarding proportion of underweight rural children, the condition in Niwai tehsil is comparatively poor with 62.9 per cent underweight children than that of Tonk tehsil with 54.3 per cent underweight children.

Table 3.9. Distribution of Underweight Children by Residence and Stratum

Particulars	Stratum I		Stratum II		Stratum III		Total	
	N	%	N	%	N	%	N	%
Niwai								
Normal	7	23.3	6	54.5	10	47.6	23	37.1
Underweight	23	76.7	5	45.5	11	52.4	39	62.9
Total	30	100.0	11	100.0	21	100.0	62	100.0
Tonk								
Normal	15	35.7	13	54.2	9	60.0	37	45.7
Underweight	27	64.3	11	45.8	6	40.0	44	54.3
Total	42	100.0	24	100.0	15	100.0	81	100.0
All								
Normal	22	30.6	19	54.3	19	52.8	60	42.0
Underweight	50	69.4	16	45.7	17	47.2	83	58.0
Total	72	100.0	35	100.0	36	100.0	143	100.0

1.4 Statistical Analysis

A. Setting Probable Limits of Proportion of Underweight Children (PUC) in the Population

Underweight Children in the Sample : 54.95% (111 out of 202)

S.E. of number of underweight children : 7.071

Probable limits of underweight children out of 202 : $np \pm 3\sqrt{npq}$

= 111± 21.213 i.e. 132.213 and 89.787 children.

Thus, out of 100 children the probable limits of underweight children are 65.45 per cent and 44.46 per cent.

B. Standard Error of the Difference between Proportions of Two Samples

(i) Is the difference between rural and urban sample significant?

Proportion of underweight children in rural sample

$$\text{or} \quad p_1 = \frac{83}{143} = 0.580$$

Proportion of underweight children in urban sample

$$\text{or} \quad p_2 = \frac{28}{59} = 0.475$$

Difference between $| p_1 - p_2 |$ = 0.580-0.475= 0.105

Best estimate of the proportion of underweight children in the universe

$$\text{or} \quad p = \frac{n1p1 + n2p2}{n1 + n2} = \frac{83 + 28}{143 + 59} = \frac{111}{202}$$

$$\therefore \quad q = 1\text{-}p = \frac{91}{202}$$

$$S.E.\,\text{Diff}.P1 - P2 \sqrt{p.q\left(\frac{1}{n_1} + \frac{1}{n_2}\right)}$$

$$= \sqrt{\frac{111}{202}.\frac{91}{202}(\frac{1}{143} + \frac{1}{59})}$$

$$= \sqrt{\frac{10101}{1704274}} = 0.077$$

Three times the $S.E._{Diff.p1-p2} = (3) \times (0.077) = 0.231$

Thus, the difference between the rural and urban proportions of underweight children is insignificant as it is less than 3 times the S.E. value and hence has arisen as a result of sampling fluctuations.

(ii) Is the difference between two tehsils significant?

Proportion of underweight children in Niwai tehsil

or $$p_1 = \frac{43}{72} = 0.597$$

Proportion of underweight children in Tonk tehsil

or $$p_2 = \frac{68}{130} = 0.523$$

Difference between $|p_1 - p_2| = 0.597 - .523 = 0.074$

Best estimate of the proportion of underweight children in the universe

or $$p = \frac{n1p1 + n2p2}{n1 + n2} == \frac{43 + 68}{72 + 130} = \frac{111}{202}$$

$\therefore$ $$q = 1 - p = \frac{91}{202}$$

$$S.E.\,\text{Diff}.\text{P}1 - \text{P}2 \sqrt{p.q(\frac{1}{n1} + \frac{1}{n2})}$$

$$= \sqrt{\frac{111}{202} \cdot \frac{91}{202} (\frac{1}{72} + \frac{1}{130})}$$

$$= \sqrt{\frac{10101}{1890720}} = 0.073$$

Three times the $S.E._{Diff.p1-p2} = (3) \times (0.073) = 0.219$

Thus, the difference between the proportions of under-weight children in Niwai and Tonk tehsil is insignificant as it is less than 3 times the S.E. value and hence has arisen as a result of sampling fluctuations.

(iii) Is the difference between male and female significant?

Proportion of underweight children in males

$$\text{or} \qquad p_1 = \frac{56}{105} = 0.533$$

Proportion of underweight children in females

$$\text{or} \qquad p_2 = \frac{55}{97} = 0.567$$

Difference between $| p_1 - p_2 | =$ 0.567-.533= 0.034

Best estimate of the proportion of underweight children in the universe

$$\text{or} \quad p = \frac{n1p1 + n2p2}{n1 + n2} = \frac{56+55}{105+97} = \frac{111}{202}$$

$$\therefore \quad q = 1\text{-}p = \frac{91}{202}$$

$$S.E.\,\text{Diff}.P1-P2 \sqrt{p.q(\frac{1}{n1}+\frac{1}{n2})}$$

$$= \sqrt{\frac{111}{202}.\frac{91}{202}(\frac{1}{105}+\frac{1}{97})}$$

$$= \sqrt{\frac{10101}{2057370}} = 0.070$$

Three times the $S.E._{Diff.p1-p2} = (3) \times (0.070) = 0.210$

Thus, the difference between the male and female proportions of underweight children is insignificant as it is less than 3 times the S.E. value and hence has arisen as a result of sampling fluctuations.

RESULTS - 2

Reproductive Health and its Measures

Considering world demography that is characterised by high rates of child and maternal mortality, the importance of safe motherhood practices and child survival needs no exaggeration. World Health Organisation has estimated that worldwide at least five lakhs women die every year from causes related to pregnancy and child birth. There is lack of awareness about maternal and child health care practices. Because of paucity of maternal and child health services particularly in rural areas, most of the deliveries are still conducted by untrained traditional birth attendants resulting in high neonatal, post-neonatal, child and maternal mortality. Therefore, percentages of birth unattended by trained health personnel has been chosen as a variable to reflect this aspect of health deprivation. The definition of trained personnel is broad: it includes physicians, nurses, midwives, trained primary health care workers and trained traditional birth attendants. In spite of the broad definition, many countries still record very high percentages of unattended births.

Promotion of health of mothers and children is one of the most important aspects of welfare. Health of every mother and its new born child is important. Also important is the environment where the birth takes place and the attention and care that is used for the conduct of delivery. Proper care in the antenatal period and during delivery is crucial for the good health of both the mother and the child. There is a high inverse correlation between high levels of infant mortality and low expectation of life at birth and the indicator of proportion of deliveries attended to by trained personnel. The capability to lead a healthy, well-nourished life or to give birth under safe and healthy conditions depends on access to health services. A well-functioning society provides people this basic opportunity. Thus, poverty can be measured not only directly (by lack of capabilities), but also indirectly (by lack of opportunities). In many developing countries there is a strong urban bias in the provision of health services. In Sierra Leone 90% of the urban population has access to health facilities, compared with only 20% of the rural population.

The percentages of births unattended by trained health personnel is an important input variable. The Capability Poverty Measure (CPM) uses it as a proxy for the capability of safe and healthy reproduction. For safe and healthy reproduction, the related concept which deserves attention is 'Reproductive Health'.

2.1 Concept of Reproductive Health

The replacement of the concept of 'women's health' by 'reproductive health' is yet another key contribution of the advocates of human development. The concept of reproductive health not only emphasises the strengthening of existing family planning and health programmes but also accrues dignity and basic rights to women. Earlier, the professed concern was 'overpopulation' and women were projected as 'producers of too many babies.' Overtime, there occurred refinement along the feminist principle which states that every woman has the right to control her own sexuality and reproduction without discrimination. This aims at ensuring the highest possible level of reproductive health care which is fundamental to the exercise of her reproductive rights. The new pattern refers to a woman's capability to:

(1) understand and enjoy her sexuality by gaining full knowledge of it;

(2) regulate her fertility through access to services and information;

(3) remain free of reproductive morbidity (and death); and

(4) bear and raise healthy children

According to International Conference on Population and Development, 1994, all countries have to strive to make reproductive health accessible through the primary health care system to all individuals of appropriate age as soon as possible and no later than 2015.

2.2 Indian Profile

In India, less than half of all the births are attended to by trained health personnel. The conditions in rural areas are far worse than those in urban areas. In rural areas, only 40.6 per cent of all deliveries received skilled attention at the time of delivery, compared to 83.9 per cent in the urban areas, in 1992. The proportion of deliveries receiving skilled attention varied from 97.1 per cent in Kerala, 85.3 per cent in Haryana, and 77.7 per cent in Tamil Nadu to lows of 33.2 per cent in Uttar Pradesh, 30.3 per cent in Assam, 29.2 per cent in Orissa, 27.6 per cent in Bihar and 24.6 per cent in Rajasthan. The inter-state variation in the availability of basic health care services is very large in rural areas as compared to the variation in urban areas. In urban areas, the proportion of deliveries attended to by skilled personnel ranges from over 99 per cent in Kerala and Punjab to 62.8 per cent in Bihar and 63.3 per cent in Orissa. For rural areas, this proportion differs widely between states, from 96.7 per cent in Kerala and 95.7 per cent in Punjab to 25 per cent or less in the states of Rajasthan, Orissa, Madhya Pradesh, Bihar and Assam. In urban areas, institutional facilities for delivery are available in all the districts of the country, serving as a positive factor in raising the percentage of women receiving skilled attention. Whereas in rural areas such facilities are rarely available.

It is estimated that India, which has about 15 per cent of the world's population, accounts for over 20 per cent of the world's maternal deaths. Given the current levels of fertility and mortality in India, a maternal mortality ratio of 453 per 1,00,000 live births results in a maternal mortality rate of about 55 maternal deaths per 1,00,000 women of reproductive age. This level of maternal mortality also means that about 15 per cent of all deaths of women of child-bearing age are maternal deaths. In comparison, it is found that the maternal mortality ratio in Europe is of the order of 10 per 1,00,000 live births or about 2 per cent of the Indian level. Because of the greater likelihood of an Indian women becoming pregnant, combined with a greater likelihood that she will die once she becomes pregnant, the average Indian woman is almost fifty times more likely to die of a maternity-related cause than her sisters in the industrial world.

In rural India, both medical and paramedical personnel fall grossly short of the officially recommended minimum standard. Health care services are notably less compared to other countries at similar levels of development. There is substantial variation between states, as well as within the same state over time. There are resource shortfalls in health personnel in the states of Assam, Bihar, Jammu and Kashmir, Madhya Pradesh, Orissa, Rajasthan and Uttar Pradesh. All-India Hospital Beds-Population Ratio is 7 per 10000 and has remained practically unchanged during 1981-91. There are alarming differences between rural and urban areas. The bed-population ratio was as low as 1.9 in rural areas and as high as 21.8 in urban areas in 1991. This shows a large urban bias in the provision of health care infrastructure in India.

Though in all the states, the proportion of women receiving skilled attention at the time of delivery has been increasing, the pace of change is quite slow particularly in the states of Bihar, Madhya Pradesh, Rajasthan, Uttar Pradesh, and Orissa where less than one-third of the deliveries are attended to by the skilled personnel.

2.3 Study Results

Tehsil-wise classification of births attended (Table 3.10) reveals that Niwai tehsil performed slightly better (31.9%) than Tonk (30.8%) regarding skilled attention at birth considering overall births. However, the gap between the tehsils recorded an increase while taking into account rural and urban areas separately. The proportion of attended births was 60.0 per cent in Niwai urban as compared to 49.0 per cent in Tonk urban. While the proportion of attended births was 27.4 per cent in Niwai rural as compared to 19.8 per cent in Tonk rural.

Table 3.10. Tehsil-wise Distribution of Births Attended

Particulars	Tonk Tehsil			Niwai Tehsil			Total		
	Rural	Urban	Total	Rural	Urban	Total	Rural	Urban	Total
Births Attended	16 (19.8)	24 (49.0)	40 (30.8)	17 (27.4)	6 (60.0)	23 (31.9)	33 (23.1)	30 (50.8)	63 (31.2)
Births Unattended	65 (80.2)	25 (51.0)	90 (69.2)	45 (72.6)	4 (40.0)	49 (68.1)	110 (76.9)	29 (49.2)	139 (68.8)
Total Births	81 (100.0)	49 (100.0)	130 (100.0)	62 (100.0)	10 (100.0)	72 (100.0)	143 (100.0)	59 (100.0)	202 (100.0)

The reasons given for not seeking natal care are not similar in urban and rural areas. In urban areas, maternity homes, hospitals and clinics are more widespread so there is a greater likelihood of urban women knowing about these services. In rural areas a higher proportion of rural mothers does not have time, knowledge, resources to leave immediately the village and go for getting natal care available in urban or distant area or are not permitted by their relatives to go to any medical facility.

Births are more likely to occur in medical institutions if women are under 35 years of age and are educated. Similarly, women having first deliveries also prefer to undergo in the presence of trained health personnel. Births to women belonging to scheduled castes or scheduled tribes are less likely to take place in medical institutions.

The conditions in rural areas are far worse than those in urban areas (Fig. 8). The variation in the availability of basic health care services is very large in rural areas as compared to the variation in urban areas. The availability of health services serves as a positive factor in raising the percentage of women receiving skilled attention.

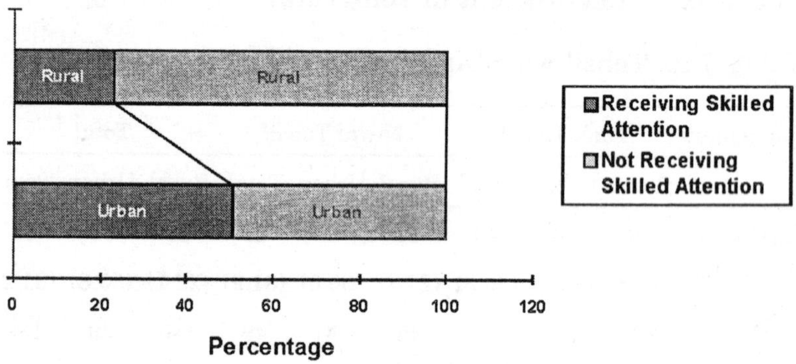

Fig. 8. Percentage of Births Receiving Skilled Attention

Out of 202 surviving children, only 63 (31.2%) received skilled attention at the time of birth while 139 (68.8%) were deprived of it. Residence-wise data indicate that among the urban births, 50.8 per cent were attended to by trained health personnel and 49.2 per cent were attended to by friends, relatives or untrained traditional birth attendants. Table 3.11 shows that in Niwai the percentage of attended births was more than that in Tonk. So far rural births are concerned, majority of them (76.9%) are unattended by trained health personnel. The proportion of rural births receiving skilled attention was relatively more in Niwai tehsil (27.4%) than that in Tonk (19.8%) tehsil (Fig. 9).

Table 3.11. Residence-wise Distribution of Births Receiving Skilled Attention

Residence	No. of Births Receiving Skilled Attention		No. of Births Not-receiving Skilled Attention		Total No. of Births	
	No.	%	No.	%	No.	%
Urban						
Niwai	6	60.0	4	40.0	10	100.0
Tonk	24	49.0	25	51.0	49	100.0
Total	30	50.8	29	49.2	59	100.0
Rural						
Niwai	17	27.4	45	72.6	62	100.0
Tonk	16	19.8	65	80.2	81	100.0
Total	33	23.1	110	76.9	143	100.0
All	63	31.2	139	68.8	202	100.0

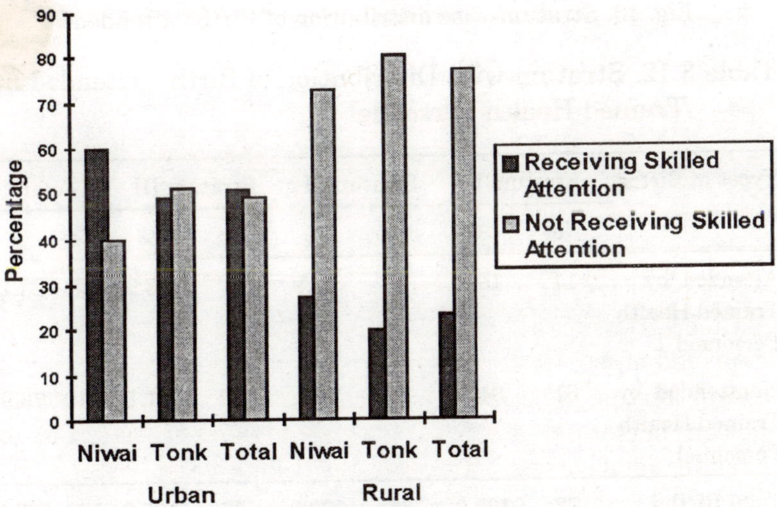

Fig. 9. Percentage of Births Receiving Skilled Attention (Tehsil wise)

In rural areas, the proportion of births receiving skilled attention has also been found to be associated with the size of the village. While in stratum I villages (Table 3.12, Fig. 10) only 15.3 per cent births were attended to by trained health personnel, in stratum III this percentage was 38.9 per cent. It may be repetitive to say that bigger villages are in comparative advantage because of the greater availability of medical and other amenities therein.

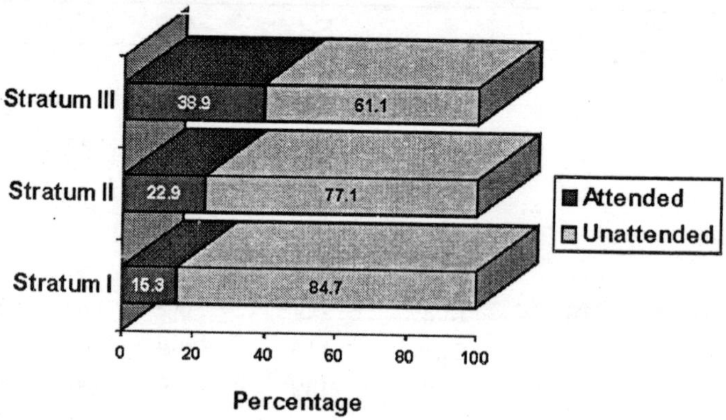

Fig. 10. Stratum-wise distribution of Births attended

Table 3.12. Stratum-wise Distribution of Births Attended by Trained Health Personnel

Types of Births	Stratum I		Stratum II		Stratum III		Total	
	No.	%	No.	%	No.	%	No.	%
Attended by Trained Health Personnel 1	11	15.3	8	22.9	4	38.9	33	23.1
Unattended by Trained Health Personnel	61	84.7	27	77.1	22	61.1	110	76.9
Total Births	72	100.0	35	100.0	36	100.0	143	100.0

Source: Field Survey.

Showing distribution of births by place of delivery, Table 3.13 indicates that in Tonk district a large majority of births (80.7%) are delivered at home and only 19.3 per cent births take place in public and private health institutions. Only 9.1 per cent births are institutional in rural areas as compared to 44.1 per cent in urban areas of the district. Results show (Table 3.14) that out of urban births, 50.9 per cent have been assisted by skilled personnel (doctors, nurses /midwives) and remaining are conducted by traditional birth attendants (dais), friends, relatives, neighbours, etc. In contrast, in rural areas, only 23.1 per cent births receive skilled attention and remaining are carried out by untrained dais, friends, relatives, neighbours, etc. This situation is not conducive to child survival and safe motherhood and results in high neonatal mortality.

Table 3.13. Distribution of Births by Residence and Place of Delivery

Residence	Public Health Facility	Private Health Facility	Own Home	Parents Home	Total
Urban	21	5	29	4	59
	(35.6)	(8.5)	(49.1)	(6.8)	(100.0)
Rural	13	0	116	14	143
	(9.1)	(0.0)	(81.1)	(9.8)	(100.0)
Total	34	5	145	18	202
	(16.8)	(2.5)	(71.8)	(8.9)	(100.0)

Note: Figures within parentheses denote the percentages to total

The most important reasons given for not seeking assistance of trained health personnel for delivery are the lack of conviction regarding its necessity, lack of resources, lack of knowledge of the services and social customs not encouraging the utilisation of health care services. These findings underline the importance of information, education and communication to promote the use of trained assistance at the time of delivery.

Table 3.14. Distribution of Births by Residence and Type of Assistance Received During Delivery

Residence Relative/ other	Doctor Total	Nurse/ Midwife	Traditional Birth Attendant
Urban	21	9	18
	(35.6)	(15.3)	(30.5)
Rural	12	21	57
	(8.4)	(14.7)	(39.8)
Total	33	30	75
	(16.3)	(14.9)	(37.1)

Note: Figures within parentheses denote the percentages to total

2.4 Statistical Analysis

A. Setting Probable Limits of Proportion of Unattended Births (PUB) in the Population

Unattended Births in the Sample : 68.81% (139 out of 202)

S.E. of number of unattended births : 6.584

Probable limits of unattended births out of 202 = $np \pm 3\sqrt{npq}$

= 139± 19.753 i.e. 158.753 and 119.247 unattended births

Thus, out of 100 births probable limits of unattended births are 78.59 per cent and 59.03 per cent.

B. Standard Error of the difference Between Proportions of Two Samples

(i) Is the difference between rural and urban samples significant?

Proportion of unattended births in rural sample

$$\text{or} \qquad p_1 = \frac{110}{143} = 0.769$$

Proportion of unattended births in urban sample

$$\text{or} \qquad p_2 = \frac{29}{59} = 0.492$$

Difference between $| p_1 - p_2 |$ = 0.769-0.492= 0.277

Best estimate of the proportion of unattended births in the universe

$$\text{or} \qquad p = \frac{n1p1 + n2p2}{n1 + n2} = \frac{110 + 29}{143 + 59} = \frac{139}{202}$$

$$\therefore \qquad q = 1\text{-}p = \frac{63}{202}$$

$$S.E.\,\text{Diff}.P1 - P2 \sqrt{p.q\left(\frac{1}{n_1} + \frac{1}{n_2}\right)}$$

$$= \sqrt{\frac{139}{202} \cdot \frac{63}{202} \left(\frac{1}{143} + \frac{1}{59}\right)}$$

$$= \sqrt{\frac{8757}{1704274}} = 0.072$$

Three times the S.E.$_{\text{Diff.}p1\text{-}p2}$ $= (3) \times (0.072) = 0.216$

Thus, the difference between the rural and urban proportions of unattended births is significant being higher than 3 times the S.E. value.

(ii) Is the difference between two tehsils significant?

Proportion of unattended births in Tonk tehsil

$$\text{or} \qquad p_1 = \frac{90}{130} = 0.692$$

Proportion of unattended births in Niwai tehsil

$$\text{or} \quad p_2 = \frac{49}{72} = 0.681$$

Difference between $| p_1 - p_2 | = 0.692 - 0.681 = 0.011$

Best estimate of the proportion of underweight children in the universe

$$\text{or} \quad p = \frac{n1p1 + n2p2}{n1 + n2} == \frac{90 + 49}{130 + 72} = \frac{139}{202}$$

$$\therefore \quad q = 1\text{-}p = \frac{63}{202}$$

$$S.E._{\text{Diff.P1 - P2}} \sqrt{p.q\left(\frac{1}{n_1} + \frac{1}{n_2}\right)}$$

$$= \sqrt{\frac{139}{202} \cdot \frac{63}{202} \left(\frac{1}{130} + \frac{1}{72}\right)}$$

$$= \sqrt{\frac{8757}{1890720}} = 0.068$$

Three times the $S.E._{\text{Diff.}p1\text{-}p2} = (3) \times (0.068) = 0.204$

Thus, the difference between the proportions of unattended births in Niwai and Tonk tehsil is insignificant as it is less than 3 times the S.E. value and hence has arisen as a result of sampling fluctuations.

RESULTS - 3

Female Adult Illiteracy

Literacy is an important aspect of capability. Illiteracy is a deprivation, not only to an individual, but also to the society. A few highly educated individuals in a largely illiterate society cannot hope to garner the benefits from knowledge for the good of society. History tells that the average level of education has to be high. Some six years of schooling seem to be the absolute minimum. Many countries are far from this situation.

The linkage between educational levels attained by different population groups and their potentialities for progress have now been substantiated by numerous studies across the world, often with special reference to women as compared to men. Equality in access to educational opportunities is particularly important for women because it is a means of enhancing income earning capacity, easing entry into public domain and improving reproductive experience and family welfare practices. Women's educational opportunities are important instruments of gender equity.

As is well known, educated women have a powerful multiplier effect on the well-being of families and on a society's general level of human development. They make a major contribution in the household and in the community. As women become literate, fertility rates fall, infant and child health improve, children's educational level increases and household nutritional and sanitary conditions improve. The right to resist injustice is something which can be practised only with certain amount of knowledge and in this way literacy helps women to resist oppression and get a fairer deal. Even for long term food security, literacy is very essential. High female illiteracy is not only a bottleneck to maintaining high growth but also to improving the general level of living of the people. Empirical evidence shows that countries with a comparable advantage in female literacy forge ahead of others. Female literacy helps contain infectious diseases, and contributes to the health and well-being of their children. It need not be emphasised that literacy is the basement for creating employability and skills. The possibility of democratic governance is substantially enhanced with a high rate of literacy.

Seeking equity in basic capabilities and opportunities is a paramount necessity in a welfare society. In this view everyone should have the opportunity to be educated, and to lead a long and healthy life. This applies in particular to women, who face substantial discrimination. Almost every set of statistics points to the harsh reality that women lag far behind whether in the sphere of literacy, enrollment, primary education, higher education or specialised skill development such as professional/vocational training. Considerable rural-urban differentials in the gross primary school enrollment ratio (PER), a flow variable, reflect low enrollments of girls (and not of boys) in rural areas.

There is wide gap in male-female literacy rates. The literacy status of females is highly worrisome in a large number of countries. Therefore, female adult illiteracy has been chosen as a constituent variable of 'Capability Poverty Measure' to capture this aspect of deprivation. This variable is noteworthy for its reflection on basic educational attainment plus information on gender inequality.

Female Adult literacy signifies the percentage of women aged 15 and above who can, with understanding, read and write a short, simple statement on their everyday life. The rate of illiteracy among women is an informative variable for assessing the general poverty situation in a country.

Educating girls, worth doing for its own sake, also has important spin-off benefits. Educated women are better able to ensure their children's survival and more likely to have fewer children. In a study of the links between education and fertility in 14 African countries from the mid-1980s onwards, secondary education yielded the most consistent benefit-invariably reducing fertility. Primary education was also frequently beneficial-with an effect in half the countries. The three recent success stories in reducing fertility - Botswana, Kenya and Zimbabwe-had the highest levels of female schooling, the lowest child mortality rates and the most vigorous family planning programmes.

A study has linked the lower mortality rates of Kerala with the remarkably high literacy rates, particularly for women, favouring the hypothesis that literacy decreases mortality levels by promoting awareness about the need and right to use public facilities including health care.

The quality of education provided also has a role to play in the level of literacy, a stock variable, prevalent in a country. In a poor quality ambience, most people educated upto the primary levels revert to illiteracy soon after they drop out of school. Sustained efforts thus need to be made to improve the quality of education, besides increasing overall levels of literacy.

3.1 Indian Profile

India has the world's largest mass of illiterate people. It is one of the least societies in the world with large rural-urban and male-female disparities. This failure is very disappointing considering the constitution which stipulates that free and compulsory education upto 14 years is mandatory and the state should ensure it. The slippage in realisation of this target, and the resultant growth in the number of illiterates, loss of productivity and the slow pace of improvement in quality of life is indeed matters of national shame. In fact, compulsory primary education is provided for in the Directive Principles of State Policy of the Constitution.

There are high gender disparities in literacy levels in India. Disparities are low, but no non-existent, in high-literacy areas. They are large in low-literacy states. Rural areas have very low levels of female literacy, with an F/M ratio of 52 per cent for rural India as a whole, and only 25-40 per cent in Rajasthan, Bihar, Madhya Pradesh and Uttar Pradesh. Even in 1991, high gender disparities persisted in Rajasthan (with an F/M ratio of only 37 per cent), Bihar (43 per cent), Madhya Pradesh (49 per cent) and Uttar Pradesh (45 per cent).

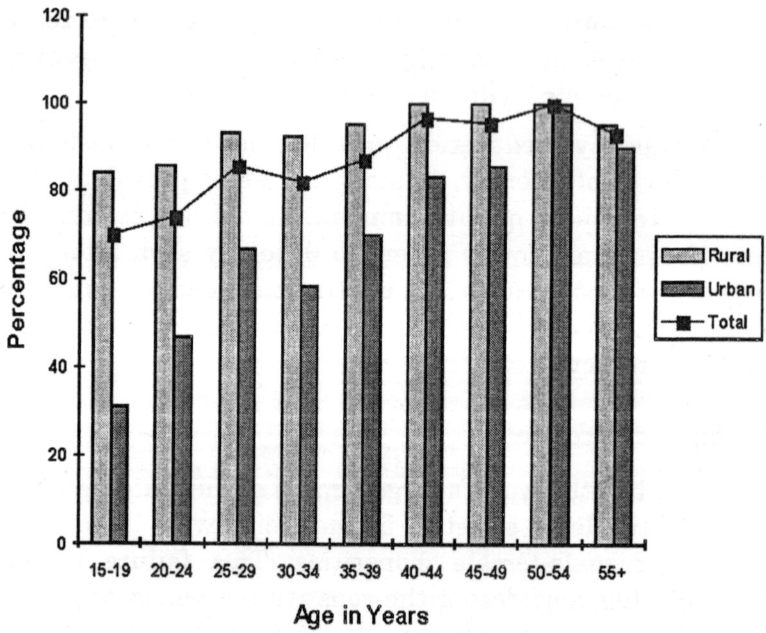

Fig. 11. Female illiterates by Age and Residence.

3.2 Study Results

There is mass illiteracy (84.4%) among the female adults. Illiteracy is considerably high in rural areas (92.2%) than in urban areas (66.0%). The total percentage of adult female illiterates is slightly high in Niwai tehsil (86.2) as compared to that in Tonk (83.5). However, the literacy percentage of rural and urban female adults is enhanced in Niwai tehsil (10.4; 35.3) in comparison to that in Tonk (5.8; 33.7) tehsil. Data indicate (Table 3.15) that illiteracy is more prevalent in old age female adults than in young ones. While in the age group of 15-19, 70 per cent of females are illiterate, in 50-54 year age group all females are illiterate (Fig. 11). It signifies that over the years there has been gradual rise in female literacy and is witnessed in both rural and urban areas. However, the change is more perceptible in urban areas. Massive illiteracy shows that there is vast scope for literacy campaign in the rural areas.

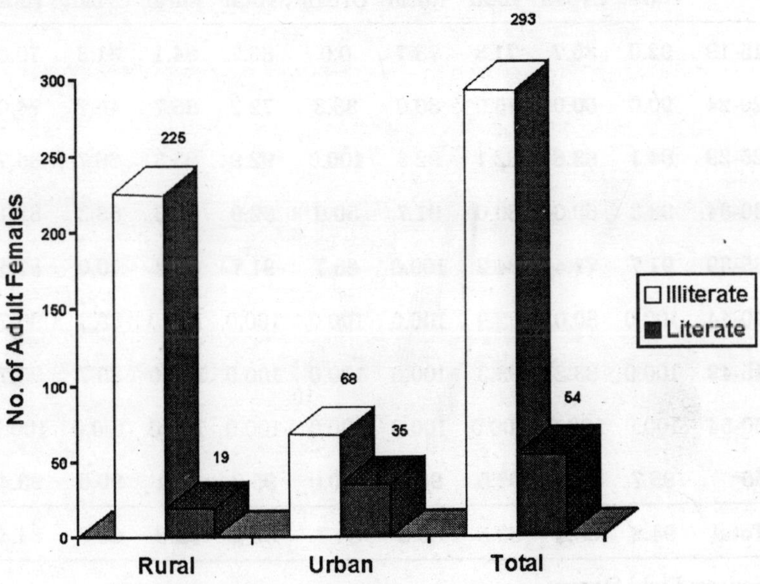

Fig. 12. Literacy Status of Adult females

Displaying factual position in numerical terms, Fig. 12 shows that out of 347 females, 293 females (consisting 68 urban and 225 rural) are illiterate and 54 literate. Age-wise classification highlights that illiteracy is very high, in females of 40 years and above than those below it (Table 3.16). Among the literate females, 6 are literate but not completed primary school, 18 completed primary school, 12 completed middle school and 18 completed above middle school. In each age group literacy is relatively high in urban females than in their rural counterparts. It also reveals that level of education in literate females is high in urban areas than in rural areas.

Table 3.15. Distribution of Illiterate Female Adults by Residence (in %)

Age	Tonk Tehsil			Niwal Tehsil			Total		
	Rural	Urban	Total	Rural	Urban	Total	Rural	Urban	Total
15-19	92.0	35.7	71.8	73.7	0.0	66.7	84.1	31.3	70.0
20-24	90.0	50.0	75.0	80.0	33.3	72.2	85.7	46.7	74.0
25-29	94.1	63.6	82.1	92.3	100.0	92.9	93.3	66.7	85.7
30-34	93.3	60.0	80.0	91.7	50.0	92.9	92.6	58.3	82.1
35-39	91.7	71.4	84.2	100.0	66.7	91.7	95.2	70.0	87.1
40-44	100.0	80.0	92.9	100.0	100.0	100.0	100.0	83.3	96.7
45-49	100.0	83.3	93.3	100.0	100.0	100.0	100.0	85.7	95.7
50-54	100.0	100.0	100.0	100.0	100.0	100.0	100.0	100.0	100.0
55+	95.7	88.2	92.5	94.4	100.0	95.2	95.1	90.0	93.4
Total	94.2	66.3	83.5	89.6	64.7	86.2	92.2	66.0	84.4

Source: Field Survey.

Table 3.16. Educational Level of Adult Females

Age (in years)	Illiterates			Literates												All Total	
				Literate < Primary Complete			Primary School Complete			Middle School Complete			Above Middle School				
	U	R	T	U	R	T	U	R	T	U	R	T	U	R	T		
15-19	5	37	42	1	1	2	2	3	5	3	2	5	5	1	6	18	60
20-24	7	30	37	1	1	2	1	2	3	1	1	2	5	1	6	13	50
25-29	8	28	36	0	0	0	1	1	2	1	1	2	2	0	2	6	42
30-34	7	25	32	0	1	1	2	1	3	1	0	1	2	0	2	7	39
35-39	7	20	27	0	0	0	1	1	2	1	0	1	1	0	1	4	31
40-44	5	17	22	0	0	0	1	0	1	0	0	0	0	0	0	1	23
45-49	6	16	22	0	0	0	1	0	1	0	0	0	0	0	0	1	23
50-54	5	13	18	0	0	0	0	0	0	0	0	0	0	0	0	0	18
55+	18	39	57	0	1	1	0	1	1	1	0	1	1	0	1	4	61
All	68	225	293	2	4	6	9	9	18	8	4	12	16	2	18	54	347

Source: Field Survey. Abbreviations: U = Urban, R = Rural, T= Total

In rural female adults, 92.2 per cent are illiterate and only 7.8 per cent are (Table 3.17) literate. As compared to this, the literacy rate is quite high in urban areas. Among the urban female adults, 34 per cent are literate. The literacy rate is relatively high in 15-34 age urban females that dips afterwards. In 15-19 age group urban females, the literacy rate is the highest (68.7%) among all the female adults in the district. This signifies that over the years there is a change in the mindset of the people and now more and more parents are sending their girl child to schools.

Spreading of educational facilities in recent decades have also helped in causing this transition. This change however, is confined to urban areas and rural literacy rate continues to be grim. Considering the national and provincial level of female literacy, the district is lagging behind and requires ample attention of public authorities to spread female literacy particularly in rural areas. District education authorities need to pay more and meaningful attention to bring about a revolutionary change in the female literacy scenario.

Table 3.17. Distribution of Adult Females by Literacy and Residence

Age (In years)	Rural						Urban						Total					
	Literates		Illiterates		Total		Literates		Illiterates		Total		Literates		Illiterates		Total	
	N	%	N	%	N	%	N	%	N	%	N	%	N	%	N	%	N	%
15-19	7	15.9	37	84.1	44	100.0	11	68.7	5	31.3	16	100.0	18	30.0	42	70.0	60	100.0
20-24	5	14.3	30	85.7	35	100.0	8	53.3	7	46.7	15	100.0	13	26.0	37	74.0	50	100.0
25-29	2	6.7	28	93.3	30	100.0	4	33.3	8	66.7	12	100.0	6	14.3	36	85.7	42	100.0
30-34	2	7.4	25	92.6	27	100.0	5	41.7	7	58.3	12	100.0	7	17.9	32	82.1	39	100.0
35-39	1	4.8	20	95.2	21	100.0	3	30.0	7	70.0	10	100.0	4	12.9	27	87.1	31	100.0
40-44	0	0.0	17	100.0	17	100.0	1	16.7	5	83.3	6	100.0	1	4.3	22	95.7	23	100.0
45-49	0	0.0	16	100.0	16	100.0	1	14.3	6	85.7	7	100.0	1	4.3	22	95.7	23	100.0
50-54	0	0.0	13	100.0	13	100.0	0	0.0	5	100.0	5	100.0	0	0.0	18	100.0	18	100.0
55+	2	4.9	39	95.1	41	100.0	2	10.0	18	90.0	20	100.0	4	6.6	57	93.4	61	100.0
Total	19	7.8	225	92.2	244	100.0	35	34.0	68	66.0	103	100.0	54	15.6	293	84.4	347	100.0

Source: Field Survey.

The main reason for the very poor literacy status of females in stratum I villages (Table 3.18) is educational in accessibility. Due to low income resources, parents prefer to keep their girl child at home for help in domestic work. Educational facilities are rarely available in these areas. Lack of transportation and unsafe rural environment are among the major reasons for the low female literacy. In stratum I villages, only 3.3% female adults are literate and 96.7 per cent are illiterate. Tehsil-wise, the percentage of literate female adults is 1.5 in Tonk tehsil's stratum I villages as compared to 5.5 in Niwai tehsil's stratum I villages. Majority of these villages are away from road sides and deprived of many amenities. The percentage of literacy in stratum II villages is 8.8 which figures at 15.6 for stratum III villages. Thus, among villages, the literacy position is comparatively worse in small villages (Fig. 13).

Table 3.18. Stratum-wise Distribution of Literacy Status of Rural Adult Females

Particulars	Stratum I		Stratum II		Stratum III		Total	
	N	%	N	%	N	%	N	%
Niwai								
Literates	3	5.5	2	11.8	6	17.6	11	10.4
Illiterates	52	94.5	15	88.2	28	82.4	95	89.6
Total	55	100.0	17	100.0	34	100.0	106	100.0
Tonk								
Literates	1	1.5	3	7.5	4	13.3	8	5.8
Illiterates	67	98.5	37	92.5	26	86.7	130	94.2
Total	68	100.0	40	100.0	30	100.0	138	100.0
All								
Literates	4	3.3	5	8.8	10	15.6	19	7.8
Illiterates	119	96.7	52	91.2	54	84.4	225	92.2
Total	123	100.0	57	100.0	64	100.0	244	100.0

Source: Field Survey

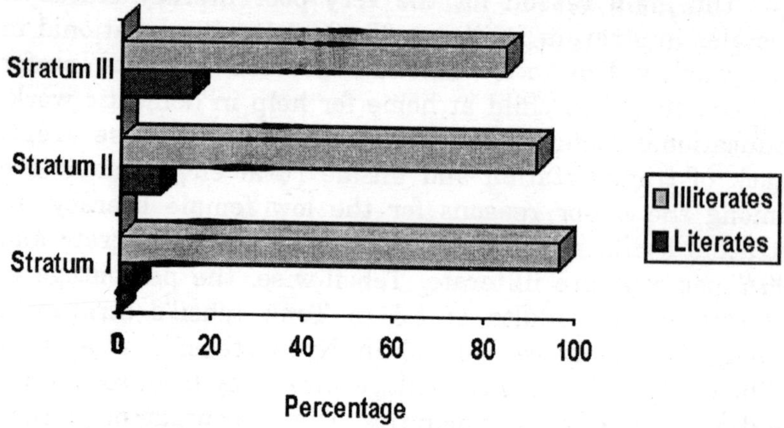

Fig. 13. Stratum-wise distribution of Literacy Status of Rural Adult Females

It has been found that teachers in government schools pay residual attention to teaching particularly in villages. The main reason for this is their accountability to government officials who bother least about the quality of teaching.

3.3 Statistical Analysis

A. Setting Probable Limits of Proportion of Illiterate Female Adults (PIFA) in the Population

Illiterate Female Adults in the Sample : 84.44% (293 out of 347)

S.E. of number of Illiterate Female Adults : 6.584

Probable limits of Illiterate Female Adults out of 347 $= np \pm 3\sqrt{npq}$ = 293± 20.258 i.e. 313.258 and 272.742 illiterate female adults

Thus, out of 100 female adults probable limits of illiterate female adults are 90.28 per cent and 78.6 per cent.

B. Standard Error of the Difference between Proportions of Two Samples

(i) Is the difference between rural and urban samples significant?

Proportion of illiterate female adults in urban sample

$$\text{or} \quad p_1 = \frac{35}{103} = 0.34$$

Proportion of illiterate female adults in rural sample

$$\text{or} \quad p_2 = \frac{19}{244} = 0.078$$

Difference between $| p_1 - p_2 | = 0.34 - 0.078 = 0.262$

Best estimate of the proportion of illiterate female adults in the universe

$$\text{or} \quad p = \frac{n1p1 + n2p2}{n1 + n2} = \frac{35+19}{103+244} = \frac{54}{347}$$

$$\therefore \quad q = 1\text{-}p = \frac{293}{347}$$

$$S.E.\,\text{Diff}.P1 - P2 \sqrt{p.q(\frac{1}{n1} + \frac{1}{n2})}$$

$$= \sqrt{\frac{54}{347} \cdot \frac{293}{347} (\frac{1}{103} + \frac{1}{244})}$$

$$= \sqrt{\frac{15822}{8720804}} = 0.043$$

Three times the $\text{S.E.}_{\text{Diff}.p1\text{-}p2} = (3) \times (0.043) = 0.129$

Thus, the difference between the rural and urban propo-rtions of illiterate female adults is significant being higher than 3 times the S.E. value.

(ii) Is the difference between two tehsils significant?

Proportion of illiterate female adults in Tonk tehsil

or $$p_1 = \frac{37}{224} = 0.165$$

Proportion of illiterate female adults in Niwai tehsil

or $$p_2 = \frac{17}{123} = 0.138$$

Difference between $| p_1 - p_2 |$ = 0.165-0.138 = 0.027

Best estimate of the proportion of illiterate female adults in theuniverse

or $$p = \frac{n1p1 + n2p2}{n1 + n2} == \frac{37+17}{224+123} = \frac{54}{347}$$

$$\therefore \quad q = 1\text{-}p = \frac{293}{347}$$

$$S.E.\,\text{Diff}.P1 - P2 \sqrt{p.q\left(\frac{1}{n_1} + \frac{1}{n_2}\right)}$$

$$= \sqrt{\frac{54}{347} \cdot \frac{293}{202} \left(\frac{1}{224} + \frac{1}{123}\right)}$$

$$= \sqrt{\frac{15822}{8720804}} = 0.041$$

Three times the $S.E._{\text{Diff}.p1\text{-}p2}$ $= (3)\times(0.041) = 0.123$

Thus, the difference between the proportions of illiterate female adults in Niwai and Tonk tehsil is insignificant as it is less than 3 times the S.E. value and hence has arisen as a result of sampling fluctuation.

RESULTS - 4

Capability Poverty Measure (CPM)

The CPM value for the district is worked out to be 69.4, which is more than 61.5, the national value of CPM, obtained for 1993. This value is a simple average of three constituent variables namely proportion of underweight children (55%), proportion of unattended births (68.8%) and proportion of female illiteracy (84.4%). Thus, among the three constituents of CPM, the district is most hard hit by female illiteracy. Table 3.19 highlights that there is considerable rural urban gap in the capability levels of people. The CPM value for urban people of the district is 54.2 as compared to 75.7 for the rural people. What worth-noting is that urban people are ahead of the rural ones in all the three parameters. The gap between urban and rural people is the highest regarding unattended births followed by female illiteracy and proportion of underweight children.

Among rural residents also, there is a gap in the capability levels according to the size of the village they live. While for stratum III villages the CPM value is 64.2, for strata II and I it is 68.8 and 84.8 respectively.

Besides rural urban diversity, there is also intra district inequality in the peoples' capability levels. This is revealed by the tehsil's capability levels. Because of the greater urban population, the CPM value for Tonk tehsil (68.3) is less than that of Niwai tehsil (71.3). However, rural-urban comparison shows that Niwai tehsil with CPM value of 48.2 for urban and 75.0 for rural is ahead of Tonk tehsil with 55.4 for urban and 76.2 for rural areas.

CPM ranks demonstrate that peoples living in different locations possess different capability levels. Basically, the capability attainments largely depend on the availability of health, education and other essential amenities. Table 3.19 highlights that while Niwai urban has got 1st rank, stratum I villages of the same tehsil have got 17th rank. It may be added that CPM reflects the deprivation prevalent in people regarding the basic minimum capabilities and indicates that as high its value is so high is the degree of deprivation. In fact, CPM is an outcome variable and reflects not only the poor capability of people but also the incompetence, sluggishness and poor allocative efficiency of government.

Table 3.19. Capability Poverty Measure

Place	Births Unattended by Trained Health Personnel (%)	Underweight Children Under Age Five (%)	Female Illiteracy Rate (%)	CPM Value	Rank
Tonk District	68.8	55.0	84.4	69.4	9
Rural	76.9	58.0	92.2	75.7	13
Stratum I	84.7	69.4	96.7	83.6	16
Stratum II	77.1	45.7	91.2	71.3	10
Stratum III	61.1	47.2	84.4	64.2	5
Urban	49.2	47.5	66.0	54.2	2
Niwai Tehsil	**68.1**	**59.7**	**86.2**	**71.3**	**10**
Rural	72.6	62.9	89.6	75.0	12
Stratum I	83.3	76.7	94.5	84.8	17
Stratum II	72.7	45.5	88.2	68.8	8
Stratum III	57.1	52.4	82.4	64.0	4
Urban	40.0	40.0	64.7	48.2	1
Tonk Tehsil	69.2	52.3	83.5	68.3	7
Rural	80.2	54.3	94.2	76.2	14
Stratum I	85.7	64.3	98.5	82.8	15
Stratum II	79.2	45.8	92.5	72.5	11
Stratum III	66.7	40.0	86.7	64.5	6
Urban	51.0	49.0	66.3	55.4	3

Source: Field Survey

To harness human potentiality for national development every effort needs to made to improve peoples' capability. Provision of basic social services and improving their accessibility to people living even in remote and difficult areas is the primary necessity in the object of bettering capability levels. Policies aimed at development of people's potential capabilities is the only prescription.

All types of government, non-government and private organisations should work together for developing the network and its optimum use.

4.1 Statistical Analysis

Setting Probable limits of Capability Poverty Measure (CPM) for the District

$$\text{Lower limit of CPM} = \frac{\text{Lower limit of PUC} + \text{Lower limit of PUB} + \text{Lower limit of PIFA}}{3}$$

$$= \frac{44.46 + 59.03 + 78.6}{3} = 60.7$$

$$\text{Upper limit of CPM} = \frac{\text{Upper limit of PUC} + \text{Upper limit of PUB} + \text{Upper limit of PIFA}}{3}$$

$$= \frac{65.45 + 78.59 + 90.28}{3} = 78.11$$

Where, PUC = Proportion of Underweight Children; PUB = Proportion of Unattended Births; and PIFA = Proportion of Illiterate Female Adults.

Thus, probable upper and lower limits of capability poverty measure for Tonk district are78.11 and 60.7.

RESULTS 5

Relationship Between Income Poverty and Capability Poverty

This section aims at establishing relationship between the income poverty and the capability poverty. Conceptually, capability is an outcome and it depends upon a number of variables. Important among them are income; accessibility of medical, health and other essential services; good household management; availability of opportunities; government priorities and intervention; efficiency of transforming income into capabilities, etc. Following analysis highlights the role and relationship of different variables with capability poverty.

5.1 Income Poverty is an inadequate explanation of capability poverty

The quality of people's lives can be poor even in the midst of plenty. Poverty is multi-dimensional. Conceptually, income poverty and capability poverty are not the same but they are correlated. Therefore, ordinarily the expansion of income is confused with the enhancement of human capabilities. According to Nobel Laureate Prof. Amartya Sen "a society's standard of living should be judged not by the average level of income, but by people's capabilities to lead the lives they value. Nor should commodities be valued in their own right-they should instead be seen as ways of enhancing such capabilities as health, knowledge, self-respect and the ability to participate actively in community life."[1] A study by Mazumdar (1990) on Asian poverty also reveals that although China is at a similar level of GNP per

[1] UNDP, Human Development Report. (1996, p.49)

capita to that of India and Pakistan, has a much better performance in terms of quality of life. Per capita GNP, therefore, cannot be taken as a surrogate for performances in quality of life.[2]

Capability poverty is broad than income poverty as it measures the denial of choices and opportunities for living a capable (tolerable) life. Poverty measures based on the income criterion do not capture deprivation of many kinds. Human development's main concern is with the range of human capabilities available to an individual, and income is relevant only in helping to enhance those capabilities.[3]

Income poverty is only a part of the picture. It uses a national 'income poverty line'. Determining the poverty line income is always somewhat arbitrary as there is no clear-cut reason for choosing one value over another. Differing opinion are expressed about the size of income that is necessary to escape poverty.

Health and education are two valuable aspects of a capable life, but income which gives "command over resources" is more a means to accomplish them. Many important capabilities, such as being well nourished or enjoying a comfortable life, depend crucially on a person's economic circumstances. Poor people also tend to be unhealthy, malnourished and uneducated. Obtaining income is certainly one of the main means of expanding choices and well-being.

5.2 Accessibility of Health Services is Important

Higher incomes also improve health. Studies in Brazil, Chile, Cote d'Ivore and Nicaragua show that an increase in household income is associated with improvements in such

---

[2] Mazumdar (1990)

[3] UNDP, Human Development Report. (1996, p.67)

health indicators as height-for-age ratios, survival rates and life expectancy at birth-and with reduced illness among children.[4]

In several studies the income effects on health appear to be larger for urban than for rural areas. It is certainly because urban areas have more health care facilities. So, although increased household income can improve health, the full benefits cannot be realised if health services are not widely available.[5]

5.3 Good Household Management Contributes to Capability Development

Household activities-though mostly unpaid and therefore, largely invisible in national accounts-contribute greatly to capability development. Women do the most-managing activity of the household, raising children, caring for the sick and elderly. In addition, their work in voluntary community organisations contributes to nutrition, health and education. Households also contribute to capability development by using their income to purchase food, medicines, schoolbooks and other means for improving capabilities.

The effects of a family's income on capability development depend not just on the size of the income but also how the family chooses to spend it. Poor households spend a large share of extra income on food. But not all goes to additional calorie consumption. Studies in Brazil, India and the Philippines show that some is used to switch to foods that are more nutritious or less monotonous or that take less time to prepare.

---

[4] UNDP, Human Development Report. (1996, p.68)
[5] UNDP, Human Development Report. (1996, p.69)

5.4 Efficiency of Transforming Income into Capabilities

Income is unquestionably important. But, it is not the level of income alone that matters-it is also the use that is made of income. A society can spend its income on arms or on education. An individual can spend its income on narcotic drugs or on essential foods. What is decisive is not the process of wealth maximisation but the choices that individuals and societies make.

Families differ in how well they translate income into capabilities. The efficiency of transforming income into human capabilities shows that similar levels of capabilities can be achieved with markedly different levels of income. Some families naturally make better use than others of higher incomes. Their choices depend partly on personal preferences and on education-and are conditioned by community knowledge and customs.

Crucial is who controls the purse strings. Several studies suggest that income is more likely to be spent on health and education when women control the cash. In the Philippines the greater the share of household income earned by women, the greater the consumption of calories and protein. In Brazil both women's income and men's improve the nutritional status of families, but women's income has an effect about seven times that of men's. In Ghana too, the greater the share of cereals under women's control, the greater households' consumption of calories.

When women have a say, money is also less likely to be squandered on cigarettes and alcohol. In Cote d'Ivorie it has been calculated that if women had as much control over cash income as men, the share of food in household spending would go up by 9% while that of cigarettes would fall by 55% and that of alcohol by 99%.

Women's control over funds also directly improve child survival. Thus, improving the position of women can have strong positive effects on their children. Many studies-including some in Bolivia, Brazil, Cote d'Ivorie, India, Kenya, Malaysia, Nicaragua, Pakistan, Panama, Peru, the Philippines and the United States-show that better education for parents, especially for mothers, increases the likelihood that their children will be educated. The effects also show up in children's health and nutritional status. In rural Cote d'Ivorie 24% of children whose mothers received no education were stunted, compared with only 11% of children whose mother had some primary schooling. And mothers education was an important contributor to the impressive health achievements by China, Costa Rica and Sri Lanka, despite these countries' low income.

Investigations of the priorities of poor people have often discovered that they put a high value on many things besides higher income-including adequate nutrition, accessible safe water, better medical services, more and better schooling for their children, affordable transport, adequate shelter, secure livelihoods and productive and satisfying jobs. Generating private income help meet some of these needs, but it certainly does not guarantee all of them.[6]

5.5 Is the Income effect on Education Considerable?

Higher incomes result in better educational attainments. As income increases, families are more likely to send their children to schools and can spend more on school materials.

But only about a third of this improvement is due to the formal education process. More important is the ability of richer families to create an environment more conducive to learning at home and at school. So, the usual way of assessing the effect of income on education-by considering

[6] UNDP, Human Development Report (19 96 pp. 49-50)

only improvements in school enrollment-may understate the benefits.

Empirical Evidence - The most widely held belief regarding India's poor educational status relates the demand for education with the poor economic status of parents. It is commonly accepted, particularly in official circles, that poor people cannot afford to send their children to school. The main 'explanation' offered is that the opportunity cost of sending them to school is very high as children make valuable contributions to the household economy. Hence, sending them to school, instead of using them as household help or wage earners, is not an economically feasible option. In addition if direct costs of education (books, stationery, uniform, etc.) are also to be borne then schooling becomes practically out of reach for the poor.

Such explanations need further probing. Is the relationship between poverty and schooling as simple and unambiguous as claimed? Is poverty the main determinant of parental decisions regarding the schooling of children? What is the relative importance of opportunity costs and direct costs in schooling decisions.

To begin with, a look at some basic facts immediately highlights ambiguities in the presumed relationship between poverty and schooling. Several third world countries, for instance, have similar or even worse levels of poverty but much better records of mass literacy than India. For instance, Zambia had a literacy rate of 76 per cent, Myanmar 82 per cent, and Tanzania 65.5.[7] While all these countries have lower per capita incomes than India, the literacy rate in India was much lower at 43 per cent. There are also a number of countries that are not far ahead of India in terms of per capita GNP, but have much higher literacy levels, such as Vietnam (88 per cent), Indonesia (77

[7] UNDP, Human Development Report. (1996)

per cent), Sri Lanka (88 per cent) and China (73 per cent). Within India itself a comparison of the poverty levels and educational achievements of, say, Kerala and Uttar Pradesh (UP) also defies the claim that it is merely poverty that prevents the poor from sending their children to school. While poverty levels, as measured by the proportion of people below the poverty line, are similar in both states (e.g. 44 per cent and 45 per cent in rural and urban Kerala in 1987-88, respectively, compared with 48 per cent in rural and urban U.P.) educational achievements in the two states are vastly different. Kerala has an average literacy rate (7+ age group) of nearly 90 per cent whereas in Uttar Pradesh the same figure is only 40.5 per cent. Furthermore, even within Uttar Pradeh, while western UP has seen a greater increase in rural incomes (relative to its eastern counterpart) this prosperity has not resulted in a corresponding increase in literacy and education. Thus, poverty is a highly inadequate explanation of regional variations in educational achievements.

There is also a fair amount of anecdotal evidence that points to the same ambiguities. Kodathuchery, a harijan village in Tamil Nadu is a particularly noteworthy example. Despite the poor economic conditions of the population-almost complete landlessness and practically no other employment opportunities-the village had achieved literacy rates of above 99 per cent for males and females in 1980. The experience of ILO's international programme on elimination of child labour (IPEC) has also shown that, even among the most impoverished families, parents are quite willing to send their children to school provided the schools function adequately. The MV Foundation in Andhra Pradesh, working with bonded labour has had similar experience.

However, this is not to deny that poverty or low income often play a role in low schooling levels. In general, poorer countries or poorer sections of the population in the same country are more likely to be found with poorer educational records. Against this general proposition, which indicates that poverty can be a potential constraint on the demand for schooling, there are notable exceptions both among countries and within India as already pointed out. These exceptions point to the fact that the poverty constraint can be alleviated or defeated by appropriate intervention most notably by improving the provision of basic education.[8]

Finally it can be concluded that capability depends on a number of input variables. The importance of income is foremost among the input variables. It is also worth mentioning that capabilities also result in increased productivity and income. Income and capabilities are positively correlated and tend to move together. This is not to say, however, that income will invariably and automatically translate into expanded human capabilities if other important factors are not in place. At the macro level also it is true to say that the link between GNP and capability development is not automatic. But that link can be strengthened through sensible policy actions. In fact, other variables provide the environment in which income plays a decisive role in the formation of capabilities. Therefore, in order to extirpate capability poverty not only the income poverty has to be vanished but also other factors have to be made productive and responsive.

5.6 Statistical Analysis

A. *Correlation between Income Poverty and Capability Poverty:* Coefficient of correlation worked out on the basis of figures of income poverty and capability poverty of different selected countries (Table 3.20) is :

$$r = 0.475$$

Where, r = Karl Pearson's Correlation Coefficient.

---

[8] Bhatty, K. (1998)

Table 3.20. Capability Poverty and Income Poverty (in %)

Country	People who are capability poor (CPM) 1993	People who are income poor (Head-count index)
Bangladesh	76.9	47.5
India	61.5	25.4
Pakistan	60.8	34.0
Guinea-Bissau	56.6	49.0
Morocco	49.7	13.1
Uganda	45.9	55.0
Indonesia	42.3	16.7
Ghana	39.3	35.9
Kenya	33.8	37.0
Tunisia	29.9	14.1
Peru	25.7	32.0
Zimbabwe	22.3	25.5
Thailand	21.1	21.8
Sri Lanka	19.3	22.4
China	17.5	10.9
Venezuela	15.2	31.3

a. Most recent year available

Source: Human Development Report, 1996

Thus, there is a moderate degree of correlation between income poverty and capability poverty. We may, therefore, conclude that, *in general,* the people who suffer from income poverty also have moderate chances to suffer from capability poverty.

B. Correlation Between Values of CPM and Per Capita Real GDP: Coefficient of correlation worked out on the basis of values of 'capability poverty measure' and 'per capita real GDP' of 101 countries (Table 3.21) is:

$$r = -0.604$$

Where, r= Karl Pearson's Correlation Coefficient.

Table 3.21. Country-wise Values and Ranks of CPM and Per Capita Real GDP

Country	Capability Poverty Measure (CPM)		Real GDP Per Capita (PPP$) 1993	
	Rank	Value	Rank	Value
Chile	1	2.8	9	8,900
Trinidad and Tobago	2	4.1	10	8,670
Uruguay	3	4.7	15	6,550
Costa Rica	4	6.1	20	5,680
Argentina	5	6.3	13	8,350
Barbados	6	6.5	7	10,570
Panama	7	7.2	18	5,890
Hong Kong	8	7.3	2	21,560
Singapore	9	7.7	4	19,350
Cuba	10	7.8	42	3,000
Korea Rep.	11	8.6	8	9,710
United Arab Emirates	12	9.9	3	20,940
Brazil	13	10.0	22	5,500
Kuwait	14	10.8	1	21,630
Jamaica	15	12.3	39	3,180
Dominican Rep.	16	12.4	32	3,690
Mongolia	17	12.6	58	2,090
Colombia	18	13.4	19	5,790
Jordan	19	14.2	27	4,380
Ecuador	20	15.0	26	4,400
Venezuela	21	15.2	11	8,360
Paraguay	22	15.9	35	3,340
Mexico	23	16.9	14	7,010

Country	Capability Poverty Measure (CPM)		Real GDP Per Capita (PPP$) 1993	
	Rank	Value	Rank	Value
China	24	17.5	50	2,330
Guyana	25	18.4	55	2,140
Sri Lanka	26	19.3	41	3,030
Vietnam	27	20.1	77	1040
Mauritius	28	20.6	6	12510
Malaysia	29	21.6	12	8360
Thailand	30	21.1	16	6350
Turkey	31	21.2	28	4210
Zimbabwe	32	22.3	56	2,100
Honduras	33	22.4	57	2,100
Libyan Arab Jamahiriya	34	22.9	17	6,125
Nicaragua	35	24.3	51	2,280
Lebanon	36	24.9	48	2,500
Swaziland	37	25.1	43	2,940
Saudi Arabia	38	25.1	5	12,600
El Salvador	39	25.6	49	2,360
Peru	40	25.7	36	3,320
Gabon	41	28.4	30	3,861
Philippines	42	28.8	45	2,590
Iran, Islamic Rep.	43	29.8	23	5,380
Tunisia	44	29.9	25	4,950
Botswana	45	30.4	24	5,220
South Africa	46	30.4	40	3,127
Bolivia	47	31.6	47	2,510
Syrian Arab Rep.	48	32.7	29	4,196
Cameroon	49	33.5	52	2,220
Kenya	50	33.8	68	1,400
Myanmar	51	34.4	96	650

Country	Capability Poverty Measure (CPM)		Real GDP Per Capita (PPP$) 1993	
	Rank	Value	Rank	Value
Zambia	52	35.1	74	1,110
Maldives	53	35.5	53	2,200
Madagascar	54	36.7	92	700
Gambia	55	38.0	73	1,190
Lesotho	56	38.6	80	980
Ghana	57	39.3	59	2,000
Tanzania, U. Rep.	58	39.4	98	630
Iraq	59	39.9	33	3,413
Congo	60	41.7	44	2,750
Cambodia	61	42.0	71	1,250
Indonesia	62	42.3	37	3,270
Egypt	63	43.7	31	3,800
Malawi	64	44.1	91	710
Sudan	65	44.3	69	1,350
Zaire	66	44.7	101	300
Guatemala	67	45.0	34	3,400
Togo	68	45.4	78	1,020
Uganda	69	45.9	81	910
Central African Rep.	70	46.0	75	1,050
Cote d'lvoire	71	46.7	63	1,620
Liberia	72	47.1	84	843
Algeria	73	49.5	21	5,570
Morocco	74	49.7	38	3270
Papua New Guinea	75	49.8	46	2,570
Senegal	76	50.9	62	1,710
Rwanda	77	51.5	89	740
Nigeria	78	51.6	66	1,540
Benin	79	51.9	62	1,650

Country	Capability Poverty Measure (CPM)		Real GDP Per Capita (PPP$) 1993	
	Rank	Value	Rank	Value
Lao Peole's Dem. Rep	80	54.6	67	1,458
Guinea	81	56.0	60	1,800
Guinea-Bissau	82	56.6	83	860
Haiti	83	57.8	76	1,050
Mali	84	59.4	99	530
Burkina Faso	85	59.7	88	780
Mauritania	86	60.8	64	1,610
Pakistan	87	60.8	54	2,160
Chad	88	61.2	93	690
India	89	61.5	72	1,240
Sierra Leone	90	62.3	81	860
Yemen	91	62.7	65	1,600
Somalia	92	63.7	90	712
Angola	93	64.0	94	674
Burundi	94	66.1	95	670
Mozambique	95	66.9	97	640
Bhutan	96	68.2	87	790
Ethopia	97	70.1	100	420
Niger	98	71.7	86	790
Afghanistan	99	72.5	85	819
Bangladesh	100	76.9	70	1,290
Nepal	101	77.3	79	1,000

Source: Human Development Report, 1996.

Thus, there is a moderately high degree of inverse correlation between Per Capita Real GDP (PPP \$) and Capability Poverty Measure. We may, therefore, conclude that, *in general,* the countries who have high Per Capita Real GDP are likely to have low Capability Poverty.

C. Rank Correlation Between CPM and Real GDP Per Capita: Rank correlation coefficient worked out on the basis of ranks of values of 'capability poverty measure' and 'per capita real GDP' of 101 countries (Table 3.21) is:

$$\boldsymbol{p} = 0.772$$

Where, p = Spearman's Rank Correlation Coefficient.

Thus, there is a moderately high degree of positive correlation between the ranks of CPM and Per Capita Real GDP. We may, therefore, conclude that, *in general,* the countries with high Per Capita Real GDP ranks are likely to have high CPM ranks.

Chapter 4

SUMMARY AND CONCLUSION

ERADICATION OF CAPABILITY POVERTY: A CRITICAL EVALUATION

India lags most developing nations in any reckoning of capability development: education, basic services and health care. Due to capability poverty persistence, much of the national resources stay unutilised, productive efficiency continues to be low, efforts to minimise population growth do not bring immediate results and superstitions keep on. By reason of competence-linked productivity losses, the economy will lag others in global markets and cannot become internationally competitive. Considering this state, a multi-pronged strategy for capability development is precisely required. The relevant socio-economic policies should focus on rectifying deficiencies in delivering social sector services and augmenting opportunities to upgrade human capability to make people educated and healthy. Access to education, health services and training in skills should go hand in hand with economic growth. The economic advancement in India should be for the people, of the people, and by the people. Following suggestions need consideration to widen and pace up the process of capability formation.

1. SUSTAINABLE HIGH ECONOMIC GROWTH

In principle, capability development and economic growth are positively correlated. People contribute to growth and growth contributes to human well-being. Economic expansion is a necessary condition for affirmative action against all kinds of deprivations. No society has in the long run been able to sustain the welfare of its people without continuous injections of economic growth. In the process of removal of capability poverty, the quantity of growth is important: without sufficient resources little can be achieved. Economic growth is significant to expand public services.

In the absence of economic growth, it is certainly possible to engineer significant short-term improvements in the level of capability development. Several countries have managed to increase public spending during periods of economic decline. Between 1980 and 1990 Nicaragua increased health spending from 3.2% of GDP to 4.9%, while GDP declined by an average 2.2% a year. But in the long term these improvements cannot be sustained without economic growth.

2. FAIR AND EQUITABLE DISTRIBUTION OF GROWTH

Quantity of growth is important but it is only one contribution to attain higher capability levels. Equally important is the distribution of growth-whether people participate fully in the process of growth. Capability formation cannot be done, therefore, by a single minded pursuit of economic growth alone. Growth has to be translated into improvements in people's lives through development of their potential capabilities. Thus, economic growth is not the end but a means to eradicate capability poverty.

But whether the additional resources are actually used tenaciously depends largely on the pattern of growth and on the distribution of private and public resources and of the rewards from growth. These factors are interdependent and are affected by government actions.

3. SOCIAL SECTOR DEVELOPMENT

India's expenditure on education and health-to-GDP ratio, at 5 per cent, is one of the lowest compared to most fast developing countries. The pace of efforts to widen the human capability base has been quite slow. At present India spends an abysmally low amount on education, about 3.5 per cent of GDP. What's worse, much of this is spent on higher education, where the rate of social subsidy is very high. Barring a few states, mostly in the south, the public expenditure on education is at the bottom of social priority list. As a nation we have spent far too little on primary education. At this rate of spending it may take many decades before we attain the East Asian levels of literacy.

The efficiency of resource utilisation too has been poor. Most of the hikes in social sector financial allocations are eaten up by payment of inflation-induced salaries of state employees. There is virtual absence of investments in adjuncts of literacy such as public libraries and other information dissemination systems, which give ultimate meaning to the acquisition of literacy skills. As a result, the continued rention of literacy skills imparted through formal schooling and various innovative measures such as non-formal education and literacy drives stand jeopardised. Policies for social sector development (mainly education and health care) and economic growth, have generally been formulated and implemented in isolation from each other.

An integrated approach is needed at every level of policy formulation and programme implementation. Who pays, who benefits and with what consequences, need to be examined for policy intervention. The strategy for development should establish linkages and promote the mutually supportive role of education and economic systems. The key is additional investment in basic education and health, and equitable access to merit goods. We must raise our education outlay to 6 per cent of GDP. Even for long-term food security, it is important that we make elementary (primary plus middle school) education compulsory, and effectively so, now. Even at 6 per cent, it would be below the level of expenditure, both as a percentage of GDP and in per capita terms, in the East Asian economies.

4. IMPROVING THE EFFICACY OF SOCIAL SERVICE PROVIDERS

So far the approach about provision and production of social services has been bureaucratic. The bureaucratic method is seen to have the effect of maximising budgets while minimising the quality of output. Each state has a bureau in charge of education which owns school buildings, recruits teachers, sets curriculum, conducts examinations and awards certificates. Similarly, another government bureau invests in hospitals, health centres and the like, and hires a retinue of doctors, nurses and health administrators to deliver the service. This manner of service delivery is a dismal failure. The state's schools and hospitals do not inspire confidence.

Thankfully, modern public administration has a way out: New Public Management. This is a fast-growing movement in public administration that applies the principles of market economics-like competition - to public services. The essence of the NPM method is to achieve a separation between 'provision' of a service and its 'production'. NPM stresses that what the state provides - including education and health- it should not produce on its own. Contracting-out; hiving-off; voucherisation - these are some of the methods that NPM prescribes. These have achieved great success all over the developed world. These methods need to be tried here as well. Because, in the end, all the grand theories of economists and political philoso-phers have to meet the touchstone of public administration.

5. CATALYTIC ROLE OF GOVERNMENT

Any strategy of human capability formation has great intrinsic value and thus in itself warrants supportive government action. Generally, households and firms base their investment decisions on private returns, which do not include the spillover benefits to those who interact with the direct beneficiaries of the investment. Therefore, market may inhibit private investment in basic social service sector. Accordingly, to rectify the market failures that tend to inhibit investments in this sector, government intervention is thoughtfully called for. By contributing to economic growth, government action can add to the material resources for capability formation. Following areas worth special focusing:

(i) Priorities and Policies

It represents a shift towards a more effective and ethical system of developing economic policy. It stands for a transformation in economic policy: focus on people, instead of commodities. Government policies can encourage pattern of growth that create jobs, increase real wages and raise market demand for human capital-and thus for the health care and education that enhance this capital. Governments can encourage private investment in human development by making loans accessible and improving information about returns. As a matter of policy, government efforts should always reflect the following:

1. The strategy for capability formation should be an integral part of reforms. The removal of all forms of basic deprivations, particularly hunger, illiteracy, poor health and sanitary conditions need strong political will for creation and expansion of opportunities and efficient management of the existing ones.

2. Because of the intrinsic value and positive spillover effects of investments in human development, governments,

acting on society's behalf, should make more such investments than individuals or households acting alone.

3. Governments should ensure that their efforts to reduce fiscal deficit do not force any cut in social sector spending.

(ii) Government Expenditure Pattern

In principle, governments in wealthier countries could give more support to human development-since the greater the GNP, the more funds available for government spending on basic social services. But this is not always so-actual spending and the way it is used vary enormously for countries with similar GNPs. Empirical evidence has shown, for example, that government expenditures on health and education have a significant effect in increasing life expectancy and reducing child mortality (technical note 4). The importance of this relationship is also evident from a cross-country study that found that per capita income and life expactancy rise together. For greater analysis, following ratios deserve special attention:

The Public Expenditure Ratio - The percentage of national income that goes into public expenditure. In developing countries it averages about 20-30% of GDP and ranges from 5% to more than 60%. This ratio depends largely on the ability and willingness of governments to collect taxes.

$$P.E.Ratio = \frac{PE}{GDP} \times 100$$

Where,

P.E. Ratio = The Public Expenditure Ratio; PE = Public Expenditure;

GDP = Gross Domestic Product.

The Social Allocation Ratio - The percentage of public expenditure (PE) earmarked for social sectors. This ratio is strongly and positively correlated with progress in capability formation. In 1993 the social allocation ratio-reflecting central government spending on health and education as a share of total central government spending-averaged about 20% for the 61 countries for which data are available. Costa Rica had the highest ratio, with nearly half its central government expenditure going to health and education.

$$S.A.\,Ratio = \frac{SE}{PE} \times 100$$

Where,

S.A. Ratio = The Social Allocation Ratio; SE = Social Expenditure (expenditure on health, education, social security, water supply and sanitation); PE = Public Expenditure.

The Social Priority Ratio - The percentage of social expenditure devoted to basic social sevices. It depends on the government's political objectives and how much it yields to the pressure of different interest groups. For a sample of 12 developing countries for which data are available, the social priority ratio-reflecting only spending on basic education and primary health care-for various years in the 1980s averages about 24%, ranging from about 11% to 55%.

$$S.P.\,Ratio = \frac{BSE}{SE} \times 100$$

Where,

S.P. Ratio = The Social Priority Ratio; BSE = Basic Social Expenditure (expenditure devoted to basic social services such as basic education, basic health care and nutrition and low-cost water supply and sanitation); SE = Social Expenditure.

Generally, the more basic social services the government supports, the better off the poor will be. In addition, following conclusions can be drawn:

1. Even if PE, SA and SP Ratios remain the same, countries can make more resources available for human capability formation purely from growth in income. In 1960 Botswana and Kenya had virtually the same GDP per capita, and for the next three decades both spent on average 9% of their GDP on health and education. But because Botswana's GDP growth rate was 6.5%, while Kenya's was only 1.6%, by 1992 Botswana was spending five times as much per person on health and education as Kenya. Fast-growing countries thus have the potential-often not realized-for strengthening the chain from economic growth to human capability formation.

2. If GDP remains constant for some years, PE Ratio can be increased by widening the tax network and thus, more funds can be made available for social priority areas. However, it is not sustainable in long term.

3. The SA and SP Ratios depend on the government's commitment to social development, as well as the demands of competing items. In some cases these items may also make a valuable contribution to human development, making it difficult to set priorities. Basic infrastructure, for example, may have a high priority because, as in the case of rural roads, it can boost the incomes of the poor.

4. Public Expenditure includes many items that do nothing for human development-and frequently undermine it. Probably the worst of these is military expenditure-which in 1994 totalled about $778 billion. Though industrial countries spent the lion's share (82%), the human development opportunties forgone because of such spending were particularly felt in poorer countries.

6. DECENTRALISATION OF SOCIAL SERVICES

In developing countries, there are large inequalities between peoples and across regions. Therefore, it is highly advisable that each type of good should be provided by a level of government that enjoys a comparative advantage in accounting for the diversity of preferences in its choice of service delivery. There are always a variety of (local) preferences and spatial characteristics, leaving the Centre with a huge information gap; it responds through non-supply, or supply of a common, amorphous package of goods and services. The Centre's tastes may disallow a multitude of public goods; especially ones whose beneficial fall-outs are regional: local transportation, forestry, street lighting, garbage removal, medicare and even local crime prevention.

In its report 'Diversity and Disparities in Human Development', the UNDP appeals for an almighty to conduit investments into backward regions and arrest ever widening imbalances. The report has data showing just how inequalities have grown. It requires actions, particularly at the following levels:

(I) policies and institutions to channel investment flows towards the rural sector, housing, social infrastructure, rural job promotion and food security. It also wants to promote equity and environmental sustainability for a growth and prosperity share-out between all regions and social groups. It urges better infrastructure, and economic incentives to penalise the exploitation of working women and children.

(II) local level mobilisation to implement location-specific poverty alleviation programmes. It also wants national and international efforts to be refocussed on pockets of low human development.

In India, big credibility gap yawn both at the Centre and in most states. Although the UNDP gives much weight to empowerment and 'distributive justice', nothing will flow to any region or target group as long as local groups are unable to demand, and monitor delivery. That would immediately necessitate 'enabling' funds for basic education, health and communications, while the Centre would naturally like to spend mostly on public goods meant for the entire country- defence for example. So the real intent of the UNDP's desires will only fructify when states themselves respond to local needs by creating independent jurisdictions that would allow private service providers, in according to market defined needs. In this regard, the third tier of government at the district, taluk and gram sabha level in rural areas and at the municipality and corporation level in urban areas has a special role to play.

7. Information Flows are crucial

Information flows are momentous to bring about revolutionary change in the human face of society. Failures in information flows often mislead the poor and the uneducated and prevent full awareness of the future returns to themselves and their children from education and preventive health care. As a result, they invest less in schooling and health care than they might if they were aware of these returns. Failures in the flow of information reduce households' incentive and ability to invest in capability. Therefore, a system for perennial flows of information is inescapable to build fertile public opinion.

8. Removal of Rural Poverty through Improved Agricultural Performance

Results show that capability poverty is rampant in rural areas particularly in small villages. Alongwith non-availability of opportunities, poor income resources are largely responsible for the deprivation. Therefore, if we want to dislodge the root cause, income poverty will have to be vanished first. From the point of view of rural poverty, many researchers argued in favour of the need for maximising agricultural growth on the ground that it will trickle down to the rural poor. Even in the absence of state intervention, a sustained process of agricultural growth could lead to a decline in the incidence of rural poverty through significant changes in the product and labour markets in favour of the poor. Higher agricultural production could lead to a fall in the prices of the commodities consumed by the poor. Again, a process of labour absorption due to growth in agricultural production, and consequently an increase in employment and wages could significantly raise the income of the agricultural labourers enabling them to spend on basic necessities *viz.* food, education, health, water supply and sanitation.

Bibliography

Bardhman, P.K. (1970): 'On the Minimum Level of Living and the Rural Poor', Indian Economic Review.

Bhatty, K. (1998): 'Educational Deprivation in India: A Survey of Field Investigations', *Economic and Political Weekly,* July 4.

Caliendo, M.A. (1981): *Nutrition and Preventive Health Care,* Macmillan Publishing Co., Inc. New York.

Dasgupta, R. (1989): *Nutritional Planning in India,* Navrang Publishers and Booksellers, New Delhi.

Epsy, M. (1996): *Nutrition,* Surbhy Publication, Jaipur.

Gupta, S.C. (1982): *Fundamentals of Statistics,* Himalaya Publishing House, Bombay.

Ghosh, M. (1998): 'Agricultural Development, Agrarian Structure and Rural Poverty in West Bengal', *Economic and Political Weekly*, Nov., 21.

Indian Council of Medical Research (1990): *Nutrient Requirements and Recommended Dietary Allowances for Indians,* Report of an Expert Group.

Kamalamma, G. (1996): *Health and Nutritional Status in India,* Aph Publishing Corporation, New Delhi.

Khanzode, V.V. (1995): *Research Methodology-Techniques and Trends,* Aph Publishing Corporation, New Delhi.

Kothari, C.R. (1988): *Research Methodology,* Wiley Eastern Limited, New Delhi.

Kothari, C.R. (1996): *Quantitative Techniques,* Vikas Publishing House Private Limited, New Delhi.

Kumar, B. (1988): *Planning Development and Poverty Alleviation,* Deep & Deep Publications, New Delhi.

Morris, D.M. and M.B. Mc Alpin (1982): Measuring the Condition of India's Poor : The Physical Quality of Life Index, Promilla and Co, New Delhi.

Mukherjee, M., J.L. Gayen and I. Roy (1981): 'A Quantitative Study of Inter-State Variation in Social Development', *Journal of Income and Wealth,* Vol 5, No 1.

Mazumdar, D. (1990): 'Poverty in Asia : An Overview', a paper presented at policy Dialogue and Pacific Development Centre, Hanoi.

Osmani, S.R. (1992): *Nutrition & Poverty,* Clarendon Press, Oxford

Parikh, K.S. (1997): 'Do We Really Care for the Poor', *Economic Times*, June, 23.

Population Research Centre, Mohan Lal Sukhadia University, Udaipur; International Institute for Population Sciences, Bombay (1995): *National Family Health Survey, Rajasthan*, 1992-93 (MCH and Family Planning).

Ravallion, Martin and Datt G. (1996): 'How Important to India's Poor is the Sectoral Composition of Economic Growth', *The World Bank Economic Review,* Vol. 10, No 1.

Shukla, P.K. (1982): *Nutritional Problems of India*, Prentice Hall of India Private Limited, New Delhi.

United Nations Development Programme (1990): *Human Development Report,* Oxford University Press, New Delhi.

United Nations Population Fund (UNFPA) for United Nations System in India (1997): 'Towards Population and Development Goals', Oxford University Press, Delhi.

United Nations Development Programme (1991): *Human Development Report,* Oxford University Press, New Delhi.

United Nations Development Programme (1992): *Human Development Report,* Oxford University Press, New Delhi.

United Nations Development Programme (1993): *Human Development Report,* Oxford University Press, New Delhi.

United Nations Development Programme (1994): *Human Development Report,* Oxford University Press, New Delhi.

United Nations Development Programme (1995): *Human Development Report,* Oxford University Press, New Delhi.

United Nations Development Programme (1996): *Human Development Report,* Oxford University Press, New Delhi.

United Nations Development Programme (1997): *Human Development Report,* Oxford University Press, New Delhi.

United Nations Development Programme (1998): *Human Development Report,* Oxford University Press, New Delhi.

Varma, M., Mathur, B., Goyle, A., Agrawal, M. and Singh, G. (1996): *Child Nutrition - Problems and Prospects,* Volume II, Ina Shree Publishers, Jaipur.

Vyasulu, V. and B.P. Vani (1997): 'Development and Deprivation in Karnataka: A District-Level Study', *Economic and Political Weekly,* Nov., 15.